The Case for Christian Apologetics

Defending the Truth of the Christian Faith in a Post-Christian and Skeptical Culture

Jefrey D. Breshears

"The Case for Christian Apologetics: Defending the Truth of the Christian Faith in a Post-Christian and Skeptical Culture"

By Jefrey D. Breshears

Copyright 2021 by Jefrey D. Breshears

Centre•Pointe Publishing. A division of The Areopagus, Inc.
www.TheAreopagus.org

All rights reserved. No part of this publication may be reproduced, stored in a retrieval system, or transmitted in any form by an means, electronic, mechanical, photocopy, or otherwise, without the prior permission of the publisher, except as provided by USA copyright law.

Cover and text layout and publishing assistance by Andrea Smith

ISBN: 9781679923821

Contents

Chapter 1:   1
The Case for Christian Apologetics

Chapter 2:   39
The Absolute Truth About Relativism

Chapter 3:
Some Common Objections ... and Some   87
   Reasoned Responses

Appendix
The Areopagus: An Introduction   125

*To my friends and colleagues in
The Areopagus,
and to all thinking Christians
who conscientiously endeavor
to love and serve God with all their
heart, soul, mind, and strength.
You are indeed the light of the world
and the salt of the earth.*

*In your heart set apart Christ as Lord.
Always be prepared to give an answer
to everyone who asks you to give the reasons
for the hope that you have. But do this
with gentleness and respect...*
– I Peter 3:15

1
The Case for Christian Apologetics

Defending the Truth of the Christian Faith in a Post-Christian and Skeptical Culture

"I must be frank with you: the greatest danger confronting American evangelical Christianity is the danger of anti-intellectualism." – Charles Malik

"The scandal of the evangelical mind is that there is not much of an evangelical mind." – Mark A. Noll

Loving God With All Our Mind

Several years ago I received a call from the minister of education in a church where I was teaching a course. He was interested to know how things were going, and I responded that everything appeared to be fine – there seemed to be quite a lot of interest, we were having spirited discussions, etc. After a minute or so he mentioned that the church staff had heard several comments about the class, but one person in particular had caught their attention when she remarked, "Dr. Breshears talks to us like we're intelligent!" The minister went on to say, "Now we [the staff] are all wondering what she meant by that. What's that supposed to say about us?" I just smiled and casually changed the subject. It seemed rather imprudent to point out any obvious implications.

If I had to choose between a clean heart or a sharp mind, I'd opt for the former without a doubt. After all, Jesus did say, "Blessed are the pure of heart" – not "Blessed are the mentally acute." But of course this is a false dichotomy and a choice that we need not make. The example of Jesus himself provides ample evidence that one does not preclude the other. Nevertheless, many Christians seem to think it is one or the other, and that a purely subjective and intuitive faith is somehow more "spiritual" than a belief system based on study and reflection. This orientation persists despite the clear warning of Scripture that "It is not good to have zeal without knowledge" (Prov. 19:2). Elsewhere in Proverbs we read that "wise men store up knowledge" and that the pursuit of knowledge and wisdom should be an absolute priority in life (Prov. 10:4; 4:7). Similarly, in II Timothy 2:15 the apostle Paul exhorts his young protégé Timothy to study diligently in order to acquire the necessary knowledge and wisdom for effective ministry, and in I Peter 3:15 Christians are enjoined to "always be prepared to give an answer to everyone who asks you to give the reasons for the hope that you have." Clearly, Scripture considers the pursuit of knowledge and wisdom to be integral to Christian discipleship.

No one should think the goal of the Christian life is to become a 'Christian intellectual' (whatever that means). Many of the most sincere and devout Christians I know are not particularly cerebral by orientation. But it is one thing to be *un*intellectual by nature – there is no shame in that – but quite another thing to be *anti*-intellectual by choice. *Anti*-intellectualism – intellectual laziness or an aversion to anything that requires mental effort – is not only unimpressive but contrary to what Jesus declared to be the greatest of all commandments: To love God with all our heart, soul, *mind*, and strength (Matt. 22:37). Does anyone seriously believe that we can honor God while living mindlessly, or practice wholistic discipleship without thinking deeply about our faith and relating it to every area of life?

Although America has always had more than its share of great thinkers, American culture in general is appallingly anti-intellectual. Generally speaking, knowledge is not highly valued – or at least, knowledge of things that truly matter. (On the other hand, many people apparently have an insatiable curiosity when it comes to the private lives of celebrities.) In a culture that values entertainment over most everything else, Socrates' dictum that "The unexamined life is not worth living" has been replaced by the notion that "The unexciting life is not worth living." This has been the theme of some of the great works in social criticism over the past ninety years from Aldous Huxley's *Brave New World* to Neil Postman's *Amusing Ourselves To Death*, Christopher Lasch's *The Culture of Narcissism* and Jacques Barzun's *From Dawn To Decadence* – all of which should be required reading for serious Christians.

The Problem of Cultural Illiteracy

Over the past several generations, due mostly to a misguided devotion to egalitarianism (or the current fad of "equity"), America has become an LCD (Lowest Common Denominator) culture in which standards have plummeted in virtually every area of life. We see this not only in our educational, political and legal systems but also in the media, popular culture, and public and private morality. Regrettably, we also see it in the church where, under the guise of "relevance," worship services are transformed into pop entertainment spectacles, homiletics (the art of preaching) degenerates into feel-good motivational rhetoric, and Christian education is reduced to fun-and-games activities for youth and mind-numbingly superficial "Bible study" for adults.

Thirty-five years ago E. D. Hirsch, a distinguished professor of English and humanities at the University of Virginia, published a book that temporarily sent the American education establishment into convulsions. *Cultural Literacy: What Every American Needs to Know* (1986) exposed the utter bankruptcy of decades of educational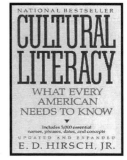

experimentation that had rendered most Americans abysmally ignorant of the basic core knowledge on which our culture is founded. Hirsch cited surveys that indicated that most college students and adults lack the basic knowledge to adequately process current events or otherwise function as informed and responsible citizens. He attributed the problem to John Dewey and other Progressive Education "reformers" who abandoned content-based learning in the early 20th century in favor of a skills-based approach that de-emphasized the accumulation of facts and knowledge, culminating in educational fads such as "values clarification" and (so-called) "critical thinking."* Predictably, the education establishment dismissed Hirsch's book as reactionary "academic fundamentalism" although in fact he was a mainstream liberal academician and no conservative.

[Note: In the early 2000's the comedian Jay Leno, host of the popular NBC late night TV program, *The Tonight Show with Jay Leno*, featured occasional "Jaywalking" segments in which he interviewed random people on the streets of Hollywood. These interviews confirmed Hirsch's thesis, only in a considerably less scientific and more humourous vein. Some examples included:

> Leno: *"Can you name two of the Founding Fathers?"*
> Interviewee: *"Founding Fathers of what?"*
>
> Leno: *"Who fiddled while Rome burned?"*
> Interviewee: *"Who fiddled? Fiddled with what?"*

---

* Regarding the emphasis on "values clarification" and "critical thinking," it should be noted that no systematic or standardized methodology has ever been established for assessing the success of such a curriculum. Certainly, there has been no effort to offer mandatory (or even elective) courses in either Natural Law theory or the principles of logic, without which "values clarification" and "critical thinking" degenerate into subjective free-for-alls. Few contemporary academicians accept the validity of traditional Natural Law, and logic is often disparaged as "Western thinking" – or in the opinion of radical feminist scholars, "male thinking".

Leno: *"Can you name any of the Ten Commandments?"*

Interviewee: *"Uhhh... freedom of speech...."*

Leno: *"What was the Gettysburg Address?... Have you heard of it?"*

Interviewee (dressed in a cap and gown at her college graduation ceremony): *"Uh, yeah, I've heard of it... but I don't really know the exact address."*

Leno: *"What is the opening line of the Bible?"*

Interviewee: *"Ummm... Long ago in a galaxy far, far away?"*]

A year after Hirsch's book was released, University of Chicago educator Allan Bloom published *The Closing of the American Mind* (1987) in which he analyzed the philosophy behind the shift away from objective knowledge-based learning to more subjective values-based (or "practical") education. According to Bloom, the major reason why modern education has been reduced to skill development and job training is because it is permeated with relativistic values. In the Introduction he noted that relativism is the cornerstone "virtue" on which all modern education is built:

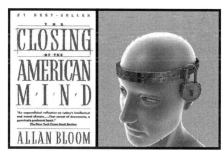

> There is one thing a professor can be absolutely certain of: almost every student entering the university believes, or says he believes, that truth is relative....
>
> [Contemporary students] are unified only in their relativism and in their allegiance to equality.... The danger they have been taught to fear from absolutism is not error but intolerance. Relativism is necessary to openness, and this is the virtue, the only virtue, which all primary education for more than fifty years has dedicated itself to inculcating. [Allan Bloom, *The Closing of the American Mind* (1987), pp.25-26.]

In a similar vein, University of Texas philosophy professor J. Budziszewski recounts his first faculty job interview (prior to his conversion to Christianity) and how his confident commitment to relativism landed him the position:

> Twenty-four years ago I stood before the [political science] department at the University of Texas to give my 'here's-why-you-should-hire-me' lecture. Fresh out of grad school, I wanted to teach about ethics and politics, so I was showing the faculty my stuff. What did I tell them? First, that we human beings just make up our own definitions of what's good and what's evil; and second, that we aren't responsible for what we do, anyway. For that I was hired to teach. [J. Budziszewski, *How To Stay Christian in College* (2004), p. 18.]

To state the obvious, such a mentality undermines real education because if everything is subjective, why bother subjecting students to the rigor of learning facts when, as Nietzsche declared, "truth" is no more than "a mobile army of metaphors." In other words, there is no truth and there are no facts – only opinions and interpretations. Or as the philosopher John Caputo of Syracuse University writes in *Radical Hermeneutics*, "The truth is that there is no truth."

Inspired by Hirsch's and Bloom's books and troubled by my own students' apparent lack of cultural literacy, I administered a 50-question exam to several hundred students at Georgia State University in the mid-1980s that covered a wide span of common names, terms, events, etc., including mind-benders such as...

- List the last four American presidents.
- What river forms the boundary between Texas and Mexico?
- What is the connotation of the term, "Wall Street" (i.e., what does it symbolize)?
- What issue was decided in the *Roe v. Wade* Supreme Court decision of 1973? and

- Who wrote the songs "Blowin' In the Wind," "Like a Rolling Stone," and "The Times They Are A-changin'?"

On a negative scale, the results exceeded my expectations. Applying a standard grading scale of 0 to 100, with 60 being the cut-off mark for a passing grade, over 90% of these students failed the test, and less than a fourth scored above the 50% mark. While nearly half could name the four former members of the Beatles, only about three in a hundred could list four current members of the U. S. Supreme Court. Almost two-thirds could identify Mikhail Gorbachev as the leader of the Soviet Union, but less than a third knew the names of Georgia's two senators. Only eight percent came reasonably close to approximating the population of the United States, with fully one-fourth estimating that it exceeds a billion. (One student was quite precise: "18.25 bazillion.") Even more troubling, 87% could not identify *Roe v. Wade* as the landmark court decision legalizing abortion.

In an article published in the *Atlanta Journal-Constitution*, I commented...

> Much has been written and discussed lately lamenting the apparent lack of knowledge regarding the fundamental core principles, institutions and traditions upon which Western civilization in general and American culture in particular are based. In 1985 Congress required the National Endowment for the Humanities to prepare a status report on humanities education as part of the NEH's reauthorization legislation.
>
> In "American Memory: A Report on the Humanities in the Nation's Public Schools," the NEH concluded that the current history and literature curriculum offered in public schools is largely inadequate, that too much emphasis is placed on mastering skills to the detriment of subject content. Among its findings, the study revealed that over two-thirds of American high school graduates were unable

to place the Civil War within the correct half-century....
[Jefrey D. Breshears, "Our Students' Minds Are a Cultural Disaster." *Atlanta Journal-Constitution* (Jan. 10, 1988, 6C.)]

This situation would be alarming enough if it were limited only to "secular" issues, but of course this is not the case. More to the point of Christian anti-intellectualism, in 2007 Stephen Prothero, a 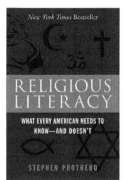 religion professor at Boston University, focused on the alarming state of religious illiteracy in his book, *Religious Literacy: What Every American Needs to Know – and Doesn't*. In the Introduction Prothero relates a comment by a visiting professor from Austria that Americans are "very religious, but they know next to nothing about religion." Prothero concluded that America, "one of the most religious countries on earth, is also a nation of religious illiterates," and confesses that early in his academic career he unwittingly contributed to this knowledge deficit:

> When I finished graduate school and became a professor myself, I told students that I didn't care about facts. I cared about having challenging conversations, and I offered my quiz-free classrooms as places to do just that. I soon found, however, that the challenging conversations I coveted were not possible without some common knowledge – common knowledge my students plainly lacked. And so, quite against my prior inclinations, I began testing them .... [Eventually] I became, like Hirsch, a traditionalist about content. [Stephen Prothero, *Religious Literacy: What Every American Needs to Know – and Doesn't* (2007), p. 4.]

In his book, Prothero pointed out that ignorance of Christianity and the Bible is not just a problem for non-Christians and secularists, and that self-described "born-again Christians" scored only slightly better than other Americans on religious literacy surveys. Other studies, such as a highly publicized survey in 2010 by the Pew Forum on Religion & Public Life, supported Prothero's bleak assessment. Even more disturbing, extensive research by the Barna Group over the past 20 years reveals that less than 10% of Americans, including the vast majority of professing Christians, hold a consistent biblical worldview.

There is, of course, an inextricable connection between cultural literacy in general and religious knowledge in particular that Christians should especially value. Neither the Bible nor Christian history and theology can be understood outside their broader historical context – just as everything that happens in Christianity today is influenced by the events of our time and the culture in which we live. This means that those with little or no historical or cultural consciousness will always have at best a superficial understanding of Scripture, Christian history and the present state of the church. Nothing that happened in history, including the life and ministry of Jesus, occurred in an historical vacuum, and it is impossible to adequately understand either the narrative or the meaning of Christ's life without some degree of historical and cultural literacy. This awareness alone should prompt Christians to value and pursue knowledge if for no other reason than to understand the Bible, the Christian faith and tradition, and the role of the church in contemporary society.

Four Causes

So who (or what) is responsible for the current deficit in religious and cultural knowledge in our society, particularly among Christians? There are four factors to be considered.

(1) One obvious source is the failure of parents to impart at least a rudimentary level of religious literacy to their children. The home should provide a rich pedagogical environment for the transmission of true knowledge, manners and morals, but regrettably many parents fail to maximize the opportunities that these formative years afford. When a child can grow up and live in a home for at least 18 years (some 157,000 hours) without learning anything substantive

about the Bible and the Christian faith (or other religions, for that matter), the fundamental responsibility for the failure undoubtedly rests with parents.

(2) For its part, public education (and much of private education) contributes to the problem by excluding religion from the academic curriculum under the misguided notion that it otherwise would violate the principle of separation of church and state. Not only is religionless education seriously deficient, but it actually promotes a secularistic worldview that is innately anti-religious.

(3) Popular culture – in particular, TV, movies, music, social media and the Internet – is a pervasive influence in American life, yet these media overwhelmingly present a critical, cynical and satirical view of the Christian faith. The anti-Christian bias in contemporary popular culture is stunning, to say the least, but in fact this has been the case throughout most of the 20th century. In 1945 C. S. Lewis commented on this problem in his essay on "Christian Apologetics" in which he reminded his audience:

> We can make people (often) attend to the Christian point of view of half an hour or so; but the moment they have gone away from our lecture or laid down our article, they are plunged back into a world where the opposite position is taken for granted. [C. S. Lewis, "Christian Apologetics," in *God In the Dock:Essays on Theology and Ethics* (1970), p. 93.]

This was of course true even in the conventional 1950s as TV, movies and music rarely acknowledged religious issues or even hinted that the Christian faith was a significant factor in American life. How often was God ever mentioned in *Leave It To Beaver* or *Father Knows Best*, or how many times were Ricky Ricardo and Lucy or Ozzie and Harriet ever shown in church? While the culture then was obviously not as explicitly hostile to Christian values as contemporary pop culture, nonetheless television, movies and music in the '50s marginalized Christianity to the point of irrelevance.

(4) The fourth factor, and in many respects the most troubling, is the current state of church-based Christian education. Several of the questions on the Cultural Literacy Quiz that I administered to my students were religious-based or had religious connotations, including...
- What is the name of the current pope, and what nationality is he? [Note: Much had been made of the fact that Pope John Paul II was Polish and the first non-Italian pope in several centuries.]
- What is the largest Christian denomination in the U.S.?
- What issue was decided in the *Roe v. Wade* Supreme Court decision of 1973?
- Who wrote most of the books of the New Testament? [Less than 20% answered "the apostle Paul" or "St. Paul," and other responses ranged from Moses, John the Baptist and Jesus to "King James" and "Nobody knows."]

Considering my students' lack of religious literacy in general and Bible knowledge in particular, I occasionally ruminated on the implications. Assuming that children can begin learning Bible stories and retaining basic Bible knowledge by about age four, and supposing that about half of my students grew up attending church at least half of the time, they would have logged nearly 400 hours in church (or 800 hours if they attended both church and Sunday School) by the time they graduated from high school. Now if students were exposed to arithmetic or English grammar or U.S. history for several hundred hours, we might reasonably expect them to know something about the subject by the time they got to college. Yet very few of my students seemed to know much of anything when it came to the Bible and Christianity. (Of course, most didn't seem to know much about history, either.)

The Case for Christian Apologetics

The troubling fact is that Christian parents are not the only ones to blame for their children's ignorance of the Christian faith. Churches also share much of the responsibility. When such things are not discussed informally and as a matter of course at home and around the dinner table, the message to children is that "religion" is merely a Sunday obligation rather than a conscientious lifestyle and a wholistic worldview. Then, when children and youth are not challenged in church to think deeply about their faith and relate it to the broader issues of life, it becomes merely a tedious ritual with little relation to the "real" world.

To some extent or another, most evangelical churches preach and teach **theology** – *what* Christians have traditionally believed about the nature and character of God, the human condition, the doctrine of spiritual salvation, and the Bible as God's unique and special revelation to mankind. But very few emphasize **apologetics** – *why* we should believe these things. **Christian apologetics (Greek: *apologia* – to provide a reasoned argument or defense) focuses on the rational and factual bases for the Christian faith – i.e., why it is reasonable to believe that the Christian faith is true**. In making the case for apologetics, I often ask Christians:

> *"Would you like to broaden and deepen your understanding of the Christian faith so as to more clearly and effectively explain and defend what you believe to both Christians and non-Christians? Very simply, that is the purpose and the value of apologetics."*

Christian apologetics is not merely an intellectual endeavor. It is intrinsically practical, and the essential purpose of apologetics directly correlates to the purpose of the gospel itself. As the 17th century philosopher Blaise Pascal put it, the purpose of the gospel is "to make [the Christian faith] attractive, make good people wish it were true, and then show them that it is." Apologetics makes the case that Christianity is a fact-based and rational belief system that corresponds to reality. In other words, the Christian faith is *true*!

There are two primary purposes of apologetics:

(1) **To educate, edify and equip believers**. To broaden and deepen the faith and confidence of Christians by providing substantiating evidence and arguments that Christian beliefs are based on factual realities and sound reason. In addition, apologetics provides a coherent explanatory system for interpreting one's own life experiences.

(2) **To engage non-believers**. To provide factual, rational and plausible answers to honest intellectual questions by honest spiritual seekers and to refute erroneous arguments and accusations by religious skeptics and cynics.

So in effect, apologetics is integral to both pre-evangelism and post-evangelism. Yet in the vast majority of churches neither adults nor young people are challenged to explore in any real depth the factual evidence and the rational reasons for what they profess to believe. Nor are they ever taught how to effectively explain and defend the basic core beliefs of the Christian faith when questioned by sincere spiritual seekers or challenged by aggressive skeptics.

Apologetics is intellectually engaging and practically useful, but it is more than that: It is a scriptural mandate and an integral part of a wholistic understanding of Christian discipleship. Throughout the New Testament we are exhorted to love God not only passionately but *mindfully*, and to be prepared to effectively explain and defend what we believe:

- Matthew 22:35-38 – "One of [the Pharisees], an expert in the law, tested [Jesus] with this question: 'Teacher, which is the greatest commandment in the Law?'

    "Jesus replied: 'Love the Lord your God with all your heart and with all your soul, and with all your *mind*. This is the first and greatest commandment.'"

- I Peter 3:15 – "In your hearts set apart Christ as Lord. Always be prepared to give an answer to everyone who asks you to give the reason for the hope that you have. But do this with gentleness and respect...."
- Colossians 4:5-6 – "Be wise in the way you relate to outsiders, and make the most of every opportunity. Let your conversation be always full of grace, seasoned with salt, so that you may know how to answer everyone."
- Colossians 2:8 – "See to it that no one takes you captive through hollow and deceptive philosophy, which depends on human tradition and the basic principles of this world rather than on Christ."
- II Timothy 2:23-26 – "Have nothing to do with foolish and stupid arguments, because you know they only produce quarrels. And the Lord's servant must not quarrel; instead, he must be kind to everyone, [and] able to teach.... He must gently instruct those who oppose him in the hope that God will grant them repentance leading them to a knowledge of the truth, and that they will come to their senses, and escape from the trap of the devil...."
- Acts 17:1-4 – "[Paul and Silas] came to Thessalonica, where there was a Jewish synagogue. As his custom was, Paul went into the synagogue, and on three Sabbath days he reasoned with them from the Scriptures, explaining and proving that the Christ had to suffer and rise from the dead. 'This Jesus I am proclaiming to you is the Christ,' he said. Some of the Jews were persuaded and joined Paul and Silas, as did a large number of God-fearing Greeks and not a few prominent women."

Furthermore, in our interactions with non-believers we must be wise and discerning. There is a time for active engagement, but there is also a time to disengage depending upon the circumstances and the guidance of the Holy Spirit:

- Proverbs 26:4-5 – "Do not answer a fool according to his folly, or you will be like him yourself. Answer a fool according to his folly, or he will be wise in his own eyes."

For most Christians, theirs is essentially a subjective, emotion-driven and/or merely inherited faith devoid of any intellectual substance. Relatively few demonstrate anything other than a superficial understanding of the Bible, and even fewer are well-versed in Christian theology, church history and apologetics. The result, inevitably, is that most cannot adequately defend what they purport to believe – even when trying to share their faith with their children. This explains why, as the Barna Group's research reveals, so many young adult Christians lose their faith when they go off to college. It also explains, at least in part, the reluctance of most Christian adults to stand up for their beliefs publicly or at work.

I am always dismayed when I hear pastors or other Christians repeat the fideistic mantra that *"We just have to believe"* some theological or moral proposition with no explanation as to *why* such a belief is warranted. If there is one problem that the church today does not have, it is that too many Christians think too much. On the contrary, a major reason why Christianity in America has been on the defensive for more than a century is that Christians have not been thinking enough. As the Yale historian Jaroslav Pelikan once noted, the church should always be *more* than a school, but the church should never be *less* than a school. But for the most part the church has been unengaged intellectually for generations, which is why we see our culture collapsing all around us today. Regrettably, the fact is that many Christians and church leaders are not simply *un*intellectual but resolutely *anti*-intellectual. The cumulative result, as the Christian philosopher William Lane Craig observes, is this:

> Churches are filled with Christians who are idling in intellectual neutral. As Christians, their minds are going to waste. One result of this is an immature, superficial faith.... The church is perishing today through a *lack* of thinking, not an *excess* of it. [William Lane Craig, *Reasonable Faith* (1984, 1994), pp. xiv, xv.]

The Scope of Christian Apologetics

Christian apologetics is based both on God's general revelation as revealed in natural philosophy and God's special revelation as revealed through biblical theology. As such, apologetics examines the validity of the Christian faith as it applies to the full range of knowledge derived not only from philosophy and theology but also the natural and social sciences – including cosmology, astronomy, chemistry, micro-biology, history, archaeology, anthropology, ethics, psychology and sociology. Therefore, apologetics deals with the most basic and important issues of life:

- Is there a God – and if so, what is the evidence?
- What is the character and nature of God?
- Is the doctrine of the Trinity rational?
- Why is it irrational to believe in a naturalistic/materialistic worldview?
- Is the Bible the divinely-revealed Word of God – and if so, what is the evidence?
- Is the Bible historically accurate?
- Is the Bible doctrinally and morally authoritative?
- Has the text of the Bible been accurately preserved and transmitted through the centuries?
- Does human life have any ultimate value, meaning and purpose – and if so, what is the evidence?
- Is morality relative , or are certain thoughts, words and actions objectively right or wrong – and if so, how can we know?
- Regarding the realities of human nature, why are human beings capable of such love, generosity and compassion but also capable of such hatred, selfishness, greed, and violence?

- Was Jesus Christ the incarnate Son of God and Savior of mankind – and if so, what is the evidence?
- Is it reasonable to believe that miracles such as those recorded in the Bible were possible and true?
- Is it reasonable to believe that Jesus Christ experienced an actual physical/bodily resurrection?
- If God is great and God is good, why is there so much evil, violence and suffering in this world?
- Is there evidence of an afterlife?

The Christian faith is not *fideism* – a mindless and irrational "leap of faith," and it is much more than just personal piety. It is also more than just a theologically-constructed belief system. Christianity is thoroughly grounded in a specific worldview and philosophy of life. **As I presented in detail in my book, *Introduction to Bibliology*, the Bible sets forth a rational philosophical and theological explanation of reality in the context of a theistic worldview that is coherent, consistent, and comprehensive.*** In that respect, it encompasses the totality of reality and addresses all the salient and perennial issues of life. Many students of the Bible begin to realize this as they delve deeper into Scripture and begin to absorb not only its metanarrative and doctrinal and moral principles but also its underlying philosophy.

All of philosophy is divided into two basic fields of study: ontology and epistemology. Ontology (or metaphysics) deals with the nature of being – in other words, the reality of what exists (both physical/material and abstract/conceptual reality). Epistemology focuses on the phenomenon of knowing – i.e., how we can know and understand the reality of what exists. Any valid worldview and philosophy should provide sensible and plausible answers to seven basic ontological and epistemological questions.

---

* See Chapter 2: "The Philosophy of the Bible" in Jefrey D. Breshears, *Introduction to Bibliology: What Every Christian Should Know About the Origins, Composition, Inspiration, Interpretation, Canonization, and Transmission of the Bible* (Wipf & Stock, 2017).

(1) Prime reality: What is the ultimate, eternal, self-existent and self-sufficient reality?
(2) Origins: Why is there something rather than nothing, and what is the source of all that exists?
(3) Human nature: What are the realities of human nature?
(4) Destiny: What happens when a person dies?
(5) The basis for knowledge: How can we know anything at all?
(6) Morality: Are good and evil objective realities?
(7) Meaning: What (if anything) is the purpose of human life?

These seven questions can in turn be reduced to four perennial issues as they affect us personally:

(1) Identity: Who (or what) am I?
(2) Origin: Where did I come from?
(3) Meaning: What (if anything) is my purpose in life?
(4) Destiny: What happens to me when I die?

Anyone who takes life seriously must concede that these are the most significant questions in life. Only a shallow and self-absorbed fool would avoid such issues. These are also the core components of Christian apologetics. **Philosophy teaches us *how* to think logically and clearly; theology teaches us *what* to think about God and life as revealed in the Bible; and apologetics teaches us *why* it is reasonable to trust the principles of natural philosophy and the doctrinal and moral truths of Scripture.**

The Consequences of Christian Anti-Intellectualism

We are often reminded that we live in a post-Christian culture, but many Christians fail to understand that we are losing the culture war (at least in part) because we have essentially forfeited the intellectual war. Ideas have consequences, and history has shown that what is intellectually respectable becomes, over time, socially acceptable and culturally normative.

In the late 19th and early 20th centuries, a few Christian leaders understood that the church, in order to uphold the credibility of the gospel, must stand up to the challenges posed by moral relativism, theological liberalism, Darwinism, Marxism, Freudianism and other threats to the faith. In an article in the *Princeton Theological Review* in 1913 entitled "Christianity and Culture," John Gresham Machen, a renowned Princeton theologian, warned that if Christians failed to adequately address the great intellectual challenges of the day, the gospel would be put on the defensive and evangelism would be seriously hampered. Machen wrote that "False ideas are the greatest obstacles to the reception of the gospel," and that passionate evangelism would experience only sporadic success "if we permit the whole collective thought of the nation" [i.e., the *Zeitgeist* – the "spirit of our age"] to fall under the influence of anti-Christian philosophies. In such a culture Christianity would become privatized, excluded from the public square, and generally dismissed as little more than "a harmless delusion." The solution, according to Machen, was for Christians to become actively engaged in the great intellectual controversies of the day and take the battle to the enemy on their own ground in the universities and seminaries. Several years later he further elaborated on the point in his book, *What Is Faith?*

> Faith is indeed intellectual. It involves an apprehension of certain things as facts; and vain is the modern effort to divorce faith from knowledge. But although faith is intellectual, it is not only intellectual. You cannot have faith without having knowledge; but you will not have faith if you only have knowledge. [John Gresham Machen, *What Is Faith?* (The Banner of Truth, 1925, 1991), p. 203.]

Unfortunately, Machen's warning went largely unheeded. Christians generally failed to respond to the intellectual and cultural challenges of the 20th century, and today we are reaping the consequences. As a result, a general lack of intellectual preparation has left many Christians confused, vulnerable and timid when it comes to defending truth. As Dinesh D'Souza observes in his book, *What's So Great About Christianity*, "Instead of engaging [the] secular world, most Christians have taken the easy way out" and "retreated into a Christian subculture." But it is a weak subculture that lacks the necessary intellectual acuity to withstand the constant pressures and unrelenting temptations of mainstream culture.

In a *Christianity Today* article in 1980 entitled "The Other Side of Evangelism," Charles Malik, a Lebanese academic, philosopher and theologian, called anti-intellectualism the greatest weakness in contemporary evangelical Christianity in that it severely undermines the credibility of our testimony. With keen and prophetic foresight and passion, Malik challenged Christians – particularly Christian young people – to take their education seriously and, regardless of their chosen vocation, prepare for a lifetime of active and effective ministry.

> I must be frank with you: the greatest danger confronting American evangelical Christianity is the danger of anti-intellectualism. The mind in its greatest and deepest reaches is not cared for enough. But intellectual nurture cannot take place apart from profound immersion for a period of years in the history of thought and the spirit....
>
> It will take a different spirit altogether to overcome this great danger of anti-intellectualism....
>
> For the sake of greater effectiveness in witnessing to Jesus Christ himself, as well as for their own sakes, evangelicals cannot afford to keep on living on the periphery of responsible intellectual existence. [Charles Malik, "The Other Side of Evangelism." *Christianity Today* (Nov. 7, 1980), p. 40.] *

---

* Charles Malik (1906-87) was a renowned Lebanese statesman and international diplomat who drafted the United Nations' "Universal Declaration of Human Rights" in 1948. Malik was also a gifted scholar, an expert on the early Church Fathers, and the author of numerous commentaries on the Bible.

The problem of Christian anti-intellectualism has been a recurring theme among evangelical thinkers in recent decades. In 1994 the historian Mark Noll of Wheaton College wrote *The Scandal of the Evangelical Mind*, alternately a survey of the rich intellectual tradition that animated evangelical Christianity in the 17th and 18th centuries and a scathing critique of the precipitous decline in the intellectual culture of mainstream evangelicalism since the mid-19th century. So impressed were the editors of *Christianity Today* magazine that they voted *The Scandal of the Evanglical Mind* their Book of the Year, but in general it did little to awaken an intellectually flaccid and lethargic church that has generally lost the ability to think. In particular, Noll was unsparing in his denunciation of pop evangelicalism as he wrote...

> The scandal of the evangelical mind is that there is not much of an evangelical mind.... Notwithstanding all their other virtues, American evangelicals are not exemplary for their thinking, and they have not been so for several generations.

> Despite dynamic success at a popular level, American evangelicals have failed notably in sustaining serious intellectual life. They have nourished millions of believers in the simple verities of the gospel but have largely abandoned the universities, the arts, and other realms of "high" culture.... Evangelicals sponsor dozens of theological seminaries, scores of colleges, hundreds of radio stations, and thousands of unbelievably diverse parachurch agencies — but not a single research university or a single periodical devoted to in-depth interaction with modern culture....
>
> By "the mind" or "the life of the mind," I am not thinking primarily of theology as such....

> By an evangelical "life of the mind" I mean more the effort to think like a Christian – to think within a specifically Christian framework – across the whole spectrum of modern learning, including economics and political science, literary criticism and imaginative writing, historical inquiry and philosophical studies, linguistics and the history of science, social theory and the arts.... Failure to exercise the mind for Christ in these areas has become acute in the twentieth century. That failure is the scandal of the evangelical mind. [Mark A. Noll, *The Scandal of the Evangelical Mind* (1994), pp. 3ff.]

In his book, *Love Your God with All Your Mind*, philosopher J. P. Moreland asks the reader to imagine a church filled with people who are intellectually shallow, self-absorbed and easily manipulated by the latest pop culture fads. As Moreland describes it, such a church would lack the theological depth, the strength of character and the necessary faith to stand against the grinding pressures and seductive temptations of contemporary life. He asks, "What would be the theological understanding, the evangelistic courage, [and] the cultural penetration of such a church?" The following points summarize his conclusions:

- It all comes down to priorities. If the cultivation of one's interior life is not a priority, there is inadequate motivation to invest the necessary time, attention and effort to develop an intellectually- and spiritually-mature life.
- Those who are intellectually lazy lack the motivation and the discipline to read and study, preferring instead to be entertained.
- If one is overly sensate in orientation, music and visual media will be more appealing than words on a page or abstract thoughts that require mental effort to process.
- If one is over-stimulated, cannot focus and is constantly hurried and distracted, he/she will have little patience for theoretical knowledge and too short an attention span to stay with an idea that is being carefully developed.

- If they read at all, self-absorbed people who are emotionally and intellectually immature will most likely gravitate toward books about Christian celebrities, the latest Christian pop fiction, or self-help books filled with simplistic moralizing and a superficial treatment of complex issues that place no demands on the reader.
- Christians who are emotionally and intellectually immature avoid substantive books that challenged readers to think deeply about the Christian faith or call them to a deeper level of commitment.
- Such a church filled with such people would be impotent in terms of standing against the powerful forces of narcissism, secularism, materialism and hedonism that dominate our contemporary culture.
- Furthermore, such a church, thoroughly co-opted by the value system of modern American culture, would offer no real countercultural or prophetic message.
- Such a church would measure her success primarily in terms of numbers – numbers that would be achieved primarily by watering-down and dumbing-down the gospel message and by catering to shallow and self-absorbed Christians.
- Eventually, such a church would become "her own grave digger," and her means of short-term success would turn out to be the very thing that would render her irrelevant in the long run. [J. P. Moreland, *Love Your God with All Your Mind* (1997), p. 93ff.]

Of course, what makes Moreland's hypothetical scenario so troubling is that it is not really hypothetical at all. Unfortunately, we don't really have to imagine such a church filled with such people because, in reality, this generally characterizes many churches and, frankly, too many church leaders. With such a mentality so prevalent in contemporary Christianity, is it any wonder why Christians are having so little impact on our society and culture? Is it any mystery why we are losing the culture war and why, with each passing decade, our society is growing increasingly rude, crude and lewd? We are not losing the culture war because the Christian belief system lacks truth and credibility. Essentially, we are losing the culture war by default. Having been co-opted by the values of our culture – not the least of which is a narcissistic, undisciplined and anti-intellectual approach to life – we have little to offer in terms of any convincing countercultural witness.

The Truth Factor

As with all religions, people identify with Christianity for a variety of reasons. Many find great psychological comfort in their faith as a source of peace, joy and fulfillment in this life, along with the belief that a loving and benevolent God will preserve their souls for all of eternity. Others take a purely pragmatic approach and hope that if there is an afterlife, their religious faith will save them from eternal hellfire and damnation. For others, it's mostly about the satisfaction they attain from the social relationships they develop in church. And of course there are always those who are motivated primarily by economic and business considerations, or even by the political advantages that church membership can offer.

But ultimately, there is really only one reason why anyone should want to be a Christian: because it is *true*. The fundamental issue is not how our faith makes us feel or the benefits it offers, but does it correspond to reality? The Christian faith makes certain exclusive truth claims that, if false, render the Christian faith fraudulent and unimportant. However, if these truth claims are true, they elevate the Christian faith to the level of infinite importance. And in order to be true, the Christian faith must be intellectually coherent, consistent and credible. In other words, it must be factual and rational. It cannot be based on subjective feelings, intuition and personal experience alone.

This is always a difficult concept to convey because people naturally want to identify with a religion in order to derive certain benefits from it. In his essay on Christian apologetics, C.S. Lewis addressed this problem with characteristic insight and bluntness:

The Case for Christian Apologetics

One of the great difficulties [in sharing the gospel] is to keep before the audience's mind the question of Truth. They always think you are recommending Christianity not because it is *true* but because it is good. And in the discussion they will constantly try to escape into stuff about the Spanish Inquisition [or the Crusades]... or anything whatever. You have to keep forcing them back... to the real point. Only thus will you be able to undermine ... their belief that a certain amount of 'religion' is desirable but one mustn't carry it too far. One must keep on pointing out that Christianity is a statement which, if false, is of no importance, and if true, of infinite importance. The only thing it cannot be is moderately important....

The great difficulty is to get modern audiences to realize that you are preaching Christianity solely because you think it is true; they always suppose you are preaching it because you like it or think it is good for society or something of that sort.... This immediately helps them to realize that what is being discussed is a question about objective fact – not about ideals and points view.... Do not water down Christianity. [C. S. Lewis, "Christian Apologetics," in Walter Hooper, ed., *God in the Dock: Essays on Theology and Ethics* (1970), p. 101.]

I am often puzzled by how entrenched fideism is in our churches and how much resistance there is to apologetics. **We are often told, "You can't argue someone into the Kingdom of God." True enough, but we also can't love someone into the Kingdom, either**. In fact, we cannot maneuver or manipulate anyone into responding sincerely and affirmatively to the grace of God. **No one comes to faith unless the power of the Holy Spirit is at work in his heart, drawing him to Christ. But what apologetics *can do***

is to break down barriers to faith by exposing and dissolving erroneous arguments and irrational prejudices against belief in Christ, and by defending the historical and philosophical integrity of the Christian faith and worldview. And that in itself makes apologetics infinitely valuable. As is sometimes (but erroneously) said of art, "Apologetics needs no justification."

One might think that for many Christians, a belief system based on evidence and reason is somehow less spiritual than a factless and irrational leap of faith. As William Lane Craig notes in his book, *Passionate Conviction*, "Sometimes people try to justify their lack of intellectual engagement by asserting that they prefer having a 'simple faith.' But here I think we must distinguish between a childlike faith and a childish faith." This is a vital distinction. A childlike faith is one that recognizes our total dependence upon our Heavenly Father. A childish faith, on the other hand, is immature, self-centered, unreflective and emotion-driven. It is all the difference between being "simple" rather than "simplistic" (i.e., simple-minded). I have always appreciated the theme of the old hymn, "Tis a gift to be simple," but I would add: "Tis a shame to be simplistic." Being created in the *imago Dei* – the image of God – we have been endowed with a mind capable of both rational and creative thought, and we should endeavor to honor God with all of our mental faculties. This is a unique aspect of the Christian faith, as B. B. Warfield, a renowned theology professor at Princeton Seminary, noted in a lecture in 1903:

> It is the distinction of Christianity that it has come into the world clothed with the mission to reason its way to its dominion. Other religions may appeal to the sword [or the emotions], or seek some other way to propagate themselves. Christianity makes its appeal to right reason, and stands out among all religions, therefore, as distinctively "the apologetic religion." It is only by reasoning that it has come thus far on its way to [supremacy]. And it is solely by reasoning that it will put all

its enemies under its feet. [Cited in George M. Marsden, *The Soul of the American University* (1994), p. 213.]

The Christian faith is all about truth. As Warfield wrote, it is uniquely "the apologetic religion." This makes it all the more imperative that we make the case for Christ using facts and reason, supplemented by our own personal experience. This is why anti-intellectualism detracts from the credibility of our message and the attractability of our faith. **On a personal level, people may like us or even admire us, but rightly or wrongly they will take us and our beliefs far more seriously if they can respect us intellectually.**

Our Calling

We live in a Lowest Common Denominator culture in which low standards and mediocrity are acceptable norms in many areas of life. Unfortunately, this is as much of a problem in many Christian families and churches as it is in our sociey in general. But scripture is clear that as followers of Jesus Christ we are called to a higher standard, and part of that high calling is to honor and serve God not only with our passion and our will, but also with our mind.

As Christians we are called to be apologists – defenders of the faith – just as we're all called to be evangelists (or witnesses) for Christ. In fact, in our multi-cultural and pluralistic society today, evangelism without apologetics is mostly an exercise in futility. In I Peter 3:15 believers are exhorted to "sanctify (or "set apart") Christ as Lord in your heart," to "always be prepared to give an answer to everyone who asks you to give the reason for the hope that you have," and to "do this with gentleness and respect." **Like the Great Commission, the call to be an apologist is not optional. This requires that we study and reflect upon what we believe so as to broaden and deepen our faith – a process that takes intentionality, commitment and mental effort.** But those who take this calling seriously find that it becomes a labor of love and that the rewards, both for ourselves as well as for others, can exceed our imagination.

The goal of the Christian life is not to be an intellectual but to be like Jesus. Spiritual maturity, not intellectual acuity, is what ultimately matters. But in Jesus we find a man who was motivated not only by love and compassion but also by truth. **In Jesus we find not only the world's greatest rabbi and mystic and spiritual guru but also the world's greatest philosopher and theologian.** As our ideal, we find in him someone who lived in perfect spiritual harmony with God the Father, and as our model, we find in him the perfect integration of passion, intellect and will.

By vocation I am an historian and an apologist, but by nature I am a contemplative Christian, and it is the cultivation of my soul and my communion with God through the internal presence of the Holy Spirit that I value the most. Nonetheless, I find that there is a synergistic relationship between spiritual formation and an active mind, and I am convinced that the two are indivisible. If we truly desire to become more Christlike, we will progressively take on "the mind of Christ" as we deepen our communion with him. The apostle Paul clearly understood this connection as he declared in his exhortation to the Christians in Rome:

> Therefore, I urge you... in view of God's mercy, to offer your bodies as living sacrifices, holy and pleasing to God. This is your spiritual act of worship. Do not conform any longer to the thought-patterns and lifestyles of this world, but be transformed by the renewing of your mind. Then you will be able to test and approve God's good and perfect will. – Rom. 12:1-2

The Solution

In this chapter I have sought to make the case for Christian apologetics. In the process, I have drawn attention to the problem of Christian anti-intellectualism, the sources of the problem, the consequences, and our calling as followers of Jesus Christ to transcend the mediocrity of contemporary status quo Christianity.

It is beyond the scope of this work to offer detailed solutions to the problem. But fortunately solutions do exist, and many excellent programs and resources are available for those who desire to broaden and deepen their commitment to Christ and their understanding of the Christian faith. For children, two programs in particular are outstanding: the Montessori-style Catechesis of the Good Shepherd (cgsusa.org) and the Bible memorization-based AWANA program (www.awana.org).

For high school and college students and adults there is a wealth of apologetical literature and resources – perhaps 90% of which has been produced in the past 25 years. At The Areopagus we offer an in-depth curriculum that includes a systematic sequence of courses in apologetics, a 6-semester series in Christian history, a 4-semester series in American Christian history, and various other seminars in contemporary cultural studies and other relevant topics. (See page 33 for a recommended reading list in Christian apologetics, and the Areopagus Seminar curriculum taxonomy in the Appendix. For a complete listing of Areopagus seminars and workshops, see our Seminar Catalogue at www.TheAreopagus.org.)

Yet despite all the impressive resources that are available in apologetics, philosophy and cultural studies, the average church-going Christian is hardly aware that this material exists. If one were to ask why this is the case, the answer is obvious: the blockage usually comes at the pastoral level. Most Christians get not only much of their information about the Christian life but also their general orientation and priorities from their pastor and church staff. But unfortunately, many pastors, youth ministers and even ministers of education often have little if any background in philosophy, apologetics, or even church history, and many are largely oblivious to all the cutting-edge research and writing that has been produced in these fields in recent decades.

Too often, pastors and other ministers still regard philosophy and apologetics as tangential to the "real" purpose of the gospel, which is saving souls. But in fact the true mission of the church is to develop disciples who love God with all their heart, soul, mind and strength, and who love others as they love themselves (Matt. 22:34-40). But even in the context of evangelism, many church leaders fail to understand that in our increasingly pluralistic and secularistic society, apologetics is inextricably an integral part of effective evangelism. The time is long-past when a Christian might prevail in a dialogue with a non-believer by simply citing Scripture as his authority because, unfortunately, there is less respect for the Bible today in mainstream society than ever before. In order to make a compelling case for Christ, it is imperative that we acquire the necessary knowledge and tactics that, to paraphrase the apostle Paul, "demolish spiritual strongholds, erroneous arguments, and every pretension that sets itself up against the knowledge of God in order to take captive every thought to make it obedient to Christ" (II Cor. 10:4-5). In this respect, apologetics is indispensable. (Chapter 3 provides several examples as it relates to the problem of relativism – the most fundamental deception of our time.)

Christians who are not content with mediocrity in their own life should not settle for it in their church. Most evangelical ministers and church staff are committed Christians who are sincerely dedicated to serving others. The tendency, however, is to think "inside the box" and merely follow the latest trends or the path of least resistance. **In a spirit of love and service, Christian parents should insist that their church provide the highest quality Christian education possible for their children and become actively involved in it.** We have only one opportunity to raise our children, and anything other than the best should be unacceptable.

Likewise, the quality of adult education in most churches should be seriously upgraded, which might require some radical changes in Sunday School and the Wednesday night schedule. Rather than the traditional Sunday School system of dividing members up into permanent self-contained classes based on age (and even sex), churches should offer creative and stimulating quarter- or semester-length courses on relevant topics related to Biblical studies, bibliology, theology, church history, apologetics, comparative worldviews and religions, contemporary cultural issues, science and the Christian faith, and literature and the arts.

If churches lack qualified teachers for in-depth and specialized courses, there are two options:

(1) Organize discussion groups around stimulating video lectures and seminars.

(2) Recruit gifted teachers in various subject fields from local universities, seminaries or other churches. Churches in a community that share their resources, including their human resources, find it to be mutually beneficial to all. As a Christian education and resource ministry in the metro-Atlanta area, The Areopagus specializes in this kind of adult education, and in most cities there are gifted Christians who are knowledgeable in at least some of the fields of study listed above who are eager to share their knowledge and wisdom within a network of associated churches.

What would be intolerable, not to mention totally unnecessary, would be to maintain the status quo. There is no reason to settle for mediocrity, and for the sake of the gospel the time has come to deal decisively with the problem of Christian anti-intellectualism. **Of all people, Christians should be the most thoughtful, the most inquisitive, and the most creative as we strive to fulfill our calling to love and honor God with all our heart, with all our soul, and with all our mind.**

And that is why Christians should study apologetics.

Notes

20 Recommended Books
In Christian Apologetics

There is a wealth of excellent apologetics literature and resources available, the vast majority of which has been produced in just the past 25 years or so. The following is not a ranked list, but simply progresses from more general works in apologetics – including an encyclopedia of Christian apologetics, an apologetics textbook, and a defense of the divine inspiration of the Bible – to more specific topics including the practical application of apologetics, the case for a Creator, the historicity of Jesus Christ and the Resurrection, critiques of atheism, cultural apologetics, and studies in science and the Christian faith. All are highly recommended.

1. J. P. Moreland and William Lane Craig, *Philosophical Foundations for a Christian Worldview* (InterVarsity Press, 2003).
2. Jefrey D. Breshears, *Introduction to Bibliology: What Every Christian Should Know About he Origins, Composition, Inspiration, Interpretation, Canonization, and Transmission of the Bible* (Wipf & Stock, 2017).
3. Douglas Groothuis, *Christian Apologetics: A Comprehensive Case for Biblical Faith* (IVP Academic, 2011).
4. C. S. Lewis, *Mere Christianity* (HarperSanFrancisco, 1952).
5. James W. Sire, *The Universe Next Door: A Basic Worldview Catalog.* Fifth Edition (IVP Academic, 2009).
6. Gregory Koukl, *Tactics: A Game Plan for Discussing Your Christian Convictions* (Zondervan, 2009).
7. J. P. Moreland, *Kingdom Triangle: Recover the Christian Mind, Renovate the Soul, Restore the Spirit's Power* (Zondervan, 2007).
8. Lee Strobel, *The Case for a Creator* (Zondervan, 2004).
9. Lee Strobel, *The Case for Christ* (Zondervan, 1998).
10. Lee Strobel, *The Case for Faith* (Zondervan, 2000).

11. William Lane Craig, *Reasonable Faith: Christian Truth and Apologetics.* Third Edition (Crossway, 2008).
12. J. Budziszewski, *What We Can't Not Know* (Spence Publishing Compnay, 2003).
13. J. Warner Wallace, *Cold-Case Christianity: A Homicide Detective Investigates the Claims of the Gospel* (David C. Cook, 2013).
14. Norman L. Geisler and Frank Turek, *I Don't Have Enough Faith To Be an Atheist* (Crossway Books, 2004).
15. Alisa Childers, *Another Gospel? A Lifelong Christian Seeks Truth in Response to Progressive Christianity* (Tyndale Momentum, 2020).
16. J. Ed Komoszewski, M. James Sawyer and Daniel B. Wallace, *Reinventing Jesus: How Contemporary Skeptics Miss the Real Jesus and Mislead Popular Culture* (Kregel Publishing, 2006).
17. Nancy R. Pearcey, *Total Truth: Liberating Christianity From Its Cultural Captivity* (Crossway Books, 2004).
18. Dinesh D'Souza, *What's So Great About Christianity* (Regnery Publishing, Inc., 2007).
19. Nancy R. Pearcey and Charles B. Thaxton, *The Soul of Science: Christian Faith and Natural Philosophy* (Crossway Books, 1994).
20. Jay Richards, ed., *God and Evolution* (Discovery Institute Press, 2010).

Questions for Reflection and Discussion

1. What is the thesis (main point) of this chapter?
2. Which point in this chapter affected you the most, and why?
3. In what areas of American life have standards declined in recent decades?
4. Why is it imperative that Christians be culturally-literate?
5. Which of the four causes of religious and cultural illiteracy have been most problematic in your life, and why?
6. What is the connection between theology (i.e., Christian doctrines and teachings) and apologetics?
7. How do your relate and respond to the quote by William Lane Craig on page 16?
8. What is your reaction to the quote by Charles Malik on page 20 and the quote by Mark Noll on pages 21-22?
9. Assess your own church in light of the comments by J. P. Moreland on pages 22-23.
10. What is the main point of the C. S. Lewis quote on page 25?
11. Why is Christian apologetics so essential to effective evangelism in contemporary America?
12. Does your church make substantive Christian education a priority? What other programs and activities take precedence over education in your church? Where should quality Christian education rank on the priority scale, and why?

Notes

Notes

Notes

2
The Absolute Truth About Relativism
The Foundational Deception of Our Time

"Jesus replied, 'For this reason I was born, and for this reason I came into the world – to testify to the truth....' Pilate asked, 'What is truth?'" – John 18:37-38

"We have now sunk to a depth at which restatement of the obvious is the first duty of intelligent men."
– George Orwell

First Things

Twenty years ago I took a friend's 23-year-old son to an Atlanta Braves baseball game. Having been born and raised in France, he was, of course, seriously culturally-deprived. He had never seen a baseball game before, and as we entered the stadium and took our seats, he was obviously fascinated by the spectacle. As much as anything, he found the architecture of the stadium and the layout of the field quite intriguing. For the first several innings I did my best to inculcate him in baseball culture, pointing out who the players were, what was happening down on the field, etc., and he nodded affirmatively with each observation. About mid-way through the game a scenario developed on the field that prompted me to lean over and remark, "Now watch this. This is an ideal situation for a hit-and-run."

Naturally, he had never heard of such a thing, and as I began to explain what I was referring to, he suddenly pointed toward the field and asked, "What's that white thing?"

"What white thing? I replied.

"That white thing," he repeated, and as I followed the trajectory of his finger, I answered, "Oh! That's home plate!"

At that moment it occurred to me that perhaps I had been assuming a bit too much. For several innings I had been chatting away, casually commenting on various players and scenarios and using all the jargon familiar to knowledgeable baseball fans, occasionally explaining myself as I went along but often just assuming that he understood perfectly well what I was talking about. Then his question suddenly brought me back to reality. For over an hour I had been talking "inside baseball" and baseball strategy with someone who literally didn't know what home plate was. In retrospect, I should have started with the basics – including the concept of home plate.

There is a principle here that is fundamental to Christian apologetics. Like my friend from France who was clueless when it came to the universe of baseball, America today is full of people who operate according to the thought-forms and value systems of worldviews that differ drastically from that of the historic Christian faith. Until the past few decades one could generally assume that most Americans had at least an elementary level knowledge of our political, legal, economic and social culture, just as most had at least a rudimentary understanding of Christianity and certain Biblically-based moral and philosophical principles that undergirded American culture and Western Civilization in general. Today, however, that is a risky assumption. Ours is an increasingly pluralistic and multi-cultural society in which there is little left of any generic common culture (other than perhaps the apparent pervasive fascination with the private lives of celebrities). The result is that we can take very little for granted. If there was a time in the past when one could reasonably assume that most people shared certain values and ideals in common, those days are long gone.

No longer can Christians assume that those with whom they interact hold values and beliefs that are generally compatible with Biblical precepts. This naturally makes Christian apologetics – the defense of the Christian faith – all the more challenging as well as interesting. After all: **What good does it do to proclaim that "Jesus Christ is the Way, the Truth and the Life" if people reject the whole concept of objective truth?** Furthermore, we can no longer assume that most people share our belief in the historical reliability and doctrinal authority of the Bible, or even that they have any real understanding of who Jesus was (and is).

The relativization of values is nothing particularly new. In fact, it has been going on for generations. Commenting on the state of moral and intellectual life in the 1950s, the English novelist George Orwell declared, "We have now sunk to a such a depth that the

restatement of the obvious is the first duty of intelligent men." Obviously, the situation has gotten considerably worse over the past generation, and certain truths that used to be universally recognized and accepted because they were self-evident must now be patiently explained and methodically defended. Therefore, in contemporary Christian apologetics it is imperative that we start from the beginning – at home plate, so to speak. Specifically, this means that we must make the case for the reality of absolute truth. Unless we clearly establish this foundational premise, much of what Christians believe will sound like little more than antiquated dogmatism and bigoted intolerance to a postmodern and secular culture steeped in relativistic values.

A Pervasive Mentality

Much of classical education was based on the premise that common people possess at least a modicum of moral awareness, and that a primary task of education is to clarify and refine this moral intuition. That sounds, of course, preposterously archaic in the context of contemporary social science- and humanities-based education which is thoroughly steeped in postmodern relativism and asserts that moral-based common sense is abject nonsense. To most educators today, what used to be called "wisdom" is merely one's "belief" or "opinion." This was why "values clarification" became such a popular educational trend beginning in the 1970s. The underlying assumption is that there is no universal standard of right and wrong, and that we (individually) define morality for ourselves according to our own preferences. Therefore, whatever seems good or feels comfortable must be right – and true.

The Christian philosopher Alvin Plantinga writes that as a young student at Yale the academic culture was wonderfully stimulating, free and open in most every respect but one: Whenever the question, "What is the truth about this matter?" came up, it was usually dismissed as unsophisticated and hopelessly naive. Obviously, Pilate's question to Jesus, "What is truth?" remains an open issue and an unsolvable riddle – if not a purely rhetorical question – to most of our current crop of cultural elites.

In *The Closing of the American Mind*, Allan Bloom observes that in the diverse atmosphere of the modern university there is one thing that every professor can be absolutely certain of: virtually every student in his class believes (or at least claims to believe) that truth is relative. Or as William Gairdner notes in *The Book of Absolutes*, "Ironically, relativism has become our only absolute." Unfortunately, this kind of shallow and sophomoric thinking is not limited to the young and the relatively ignorant; it is also normative among university professors who are, presumably, paid to dispense knowledge and wisdom to their students. Writing of his first interview as a prospective faculty candidate at the University of

Texas, J. Budziszewski comments on the irony and the almost comic irrationality of the scenario:

> Twenty-four years ago I stood before the [political science] department at the University of Texas to give my 'here's-why-you-should-hire-me' lecture. Fresh out of grad school, I wanted to teach about ethics and politics, so I was showing the faculty my stuff. What did I tell them? First, that we human beings just make up our own definitions of what's good and what's evil; and second, that we aren't responsible for what we do, anyway. For that I was hired to teach. [J. Budziszewski, *How To Stay Christian in College* (2004), p. 18.]

In our contemporary culture there is a pervasive assumption that there is no absolute truth, only opinions. Furthermore, in keeping with the egalitarian ethos of our time, we are constantly reminded that everyone's opinion is more-or-less equally valid, so what right have we to judge? When Friedrich Nietzsche wrote, "There are no facts, only interpretations," most scholars of his day dismissed him as a screwball. Today, many revere him as a sage, and his view of reality has become mainstream. As John Caputo confidently asserts in *Radical Hermeneutics*, "The truth is that there is no truth."

There are two interconnected philosophical presuppositions that underlie our current *Zeitgeist* – the spirit of our time: **Relativism** asserts that objective and universal truth does not exist, while **subjectivism** redefines truth as merely the values and preferences of individuals. Perhaps the ultimate example of this mentality is the statement by Supreme Court Justice Anthony Kennedy in the *Planned Parenthood v. Casey* case of 1992 when he declared: "At the heart of liberty is the right to define one's own concept of existence, of meaning, of the universe, and of the mystery of human life." Logic and morality aside, this was an absolutely shocking expression of philosophical relativism.

The assumptions of relativism and subjectivism are widespread, and they are rarely challenged in the public square – certainly not in the media, popular culture, or within our institutions of higher learning. As a result, many confidently contend that something can be "true for you, but not for me" and that even contradictory beliefs can be equally valid. Meanwhile, those who uphold the principle of absolute truth are dismissed as narrow-minded simpletons.

Unfortunately, the illogicality of relativism has affected Christians just as it has everyone else. According to research by the Barna Group, the majority of self-proclaimed "born-again" Christians, like Pontius Pilate two thousand years ago, do not believe in absolute truth – despite Jesus' assertion that "I am the Way, the Truth, and the Life" [John 14:6], and that the purpose of his earthly mission was to "testify to the truth."

Something is seriously amiss. Our culture is swamped by relativistic and subjectivistic values, and a major contributing factor is the dumbing-down of contemporary education. **In general, our education system at every level from elementary school to graduate school fails to train people to think logically and critically. When the main focus of education shifts from critical thinking to job training, or from building a solid knowledge base to building self-esteem, it is inevitable that standards and expectations will plummet.** As a result, the greatest fear in the education establishment today seems not to be ignorance but elitism, not muddled thinking but "intolerance."

To an alarming extent this same mentality has crept into much of Christian education. Many Christian schools, colleges and seminaries have bought into many of the trendy fads of the secular education establishment, and the affects are apparent in much of what passes for Christian education in our churches. Furthermore, it will take more than the latest reforms by professional educrats to rectify what is our greatest challenge in contemporary American life: the problem of relativism and subjectivism.

In a society in which virtually all moral restraints have been discarded and in which the illegitimate birth rate, child abuse and neglect, drug, alcohol and pornography addiction, incivility, crime and other social pathologies are epidemic, it is understandable that there would be a general cynicism regarding the idea of absolute moral standards. This is particularly apparent within the realm of popular culture, which for the most part is utterly non-discriminating when it comes to both moral and aesthetic standards. In such a culture, value is defined by whatever sells or whatever is trendy and "woke". So presumably, there is no qualitative or aesthetic difference between classical music (or even classic rock) and gangsta rap and death metal, or between the music of Bach, Beethoven or even The Beatles and that of Britney Spears, Snoop Dogg or Lady Gaga. The propagandists and purveyors of cultural relativism would like us to believe that *Dumb and Dumber* or *Jackass: The Movie* are very bit as valid as *Gone With the Wind* or *Les Miserables*. As cultural profiteers, they refuse to distinguish between true art and crass entertainment because such distinctions require value judgements based on higher aesthetic and moral standards that are, in their minds, purely arbitrary and subjective.

The widespread acceptance of relativism directly affects people's views not only on morality, art and beauty, but also on religion. **Relativism and subjectivism are the critical philosophical presuppositions behind religious pluralism – the notion that all religions are essentially the same.** According to this assumption, all religions are equally valid and legitimate (or equally invalid and illegitimate) even though, in fact, they are inherently contradictory. Obviously, such a mentality renders the exclusive truth claims  of Jesus Christ to be absurd and totally unacceptable. Therefore, the religious pluralist must conclude one of two things about Jesus: either he never actually made these claims (i.e., the Bible misrepresents what Jesus said and did), or else Jesus, as an enlightened but fallible ancient prophet, was simply wrong.

The consequences of relativism can be serious if taken it to their logical conclusions. In *True For You, But Not For Me*, the Christian philosopher Paul Copan quotes a punk rocker as typical of many conflicted young people today:

> I belong to the Blank Generation. I have no beliefs. I belong to no community, tradition, or anything like that. I'm lost in this vast world. I belong nowhere. I have absolutely no identity. [Quoted in Paul Copan, *True for You, But Not For Me* (2009), p. 12.]

The Optimal Issue

Practically-speaking, the question of whether objective truth exists is the foundational issue of the Christian faith. If relativists are right and there is no truth, then all doctrines and professions of faith are purely subjective and ultimately inconsequential – in which case the Christian faith is essentially a fraud and its unique truth-claims are as ludicrous as they are arrogant.

As with all religions, people identify with Christianity for a variety of reasons:

(1) Cultural. For many, their conception of Christianity is simply that of a religion or their family heritage. To some extent or another, they value the religious institutions and rituals associated with this tradition, but otherwise it has little impact in terms of what they actually believe about life and values and reality in general. Cultural Christians typically fail to internalize the unique truth claims of the Christian faith or conceptualize their religion as a medium through which they can relate personally to God.

(2) Psychological. Many people find great psychological comfort in their faith as a source of comfort, joy, and hope. Certainly, religious faith can induce peace of mind and a sense of purpose in life, but such feelings are valid only if they correspond to real Truth.

(3) Social. Many find it beneficial to belong to a church for relational, cultural, business, or even political reasons. Church provides a social network and a circle of friendships that make life more enjoyable.

(4) Pragmatic. Many take a calculated and pragmatic approach: If there really is an afterlife and the prospect of divine judgement, they hope their religious faith will save them from eternal hellfire and damnation.

Most of these reasons have at least some value, but they all miss the main point. As I emphasized in Chapter 1: **Ultimately, the only reason for being a Christian is if in fact the Christian faith is *true*.** The fundamental issue is not how it makes us feel or the benefits it offers, but does it correspond to reality? This is why an understanding of Christian apologetics is so vitally important. Apologetics (derived from the Greek *apologia*: to offer a reasoned argument or defense) is a branch of theology. Theology deals with *what* Christians believe – the key doctrines of the faith derived from Scripture as properly interpreted. Apologetics, on the other hand, deals with *why* Christians should believe these things – i.e., why it makes sense to believe them. In apologetics we make our case for the truth of the Christian faith based primarily on two factors:

(1) Facts – evidence derived from history, the physical sciences, the social sciences, and personal experience; and

(2) Reason – rational conclusions derived from philosophy, including the basic rules of logical deduction.

Christian belief is not an irrational "leap of faith" but a sober and rational step of faith. Of course, our faith can (and should) also engage our emotions – as Jesus taught, we should love God not only mindfully but passionately – but personal subjective emotions should never drive our beliefs.

As C. S. Lewis emphasized in his essay on "Christian Apologetics," Christianity is important only if it is true. If it is untrue, it is of no value whatsoever; but if it *is* true, it is of infinite value. This is a difficult concept to convey to modern audiences who are conditioned to consider things as valuable only if they seem practical and beneficial.

One of the great difficulties is to keep before the audience's mind the question of Truth. They always think your are recommending Christianity not because it is *true* but because it is *good*. And in the discussion they will at every moment try to escape from the issue of 'True or False' into stuff about the Spanish Inquisition [or the Crusades]... or anything whatever. You have to keep forcing them back... to the real point. Only thus will you be able to undermine... their belief that a certain amount of 'religion' is desirable but one mustn't carry it too far. One must keep on pointing out that Christianity is a statement which, if false, is of no importance, and if true, of infinite importance. The one thing is cannot be is moderately important....

The great difficulty is to get modern audiences to realize that you are preaching Christianity solely and simply because you think it is *true*; they always suppose you are preaching it because you like it or think it is good for society or something of that sort.... This immediately helps them to realize that what is being discussed is a question about objective fact – not [opinions] about ideals and points of view.... Do not attempt to water Christianity down [or relativize it]." [C. S. Lewis, "Christian Apologetics," in Walter Hooper, ed., *God in the Dock: Essays On Theology and Ethics* (1971), p. 101.]

Philosopher Peter Kreeft observes that of all the symptoms of decay in our decadent culture, relativism is the most disastrous. Michael Novak concurs, and warns of the insidious effects of relativism not only on American culture but that of all free societies:

Relativism is an invisible gas, odorless, deadly, that is now polluting every free society on earth. It is a gas that attacks the central nervous system of moral striving. The most perilous threat to the free society today is... not political or economic. It is the poisonous, corrupting culture of relativism. [Michael Novak, "Awakening from Nihilism: The Templeton Prize Address." *First Things* (Aug/Sep 1994), p. 20.]

Lewis, who was not prone to exaggeration, was even more demonstrative. In his essay, "The Poison of Subjectivism," he referred to subjective relativism as "the fatal superstition that men can create [their own] values" and "the disease that will certainly end our species (and... damn our souls) if it is not crushed."

The intellectual and moral consequences of relativism and subjectivism are glaringly obvious, but no less serious is the spiritual fall-out. Relativism is fundamentally nonsensical, contradictory, irrational, and intellectually bankrupt. Errors in logic and fact can only be discovered and corrected if truth actually exists and if people are willing to be guided by it. But for those who actually believe there is no absolute truth, there is absolutely no hope. Intellectually confused, they are detached from reality and, even more tragically, mired in spiritual darkness.

A foundational presupposition of Christian apologetics – and one on which Christians should be clear and unequivocal – is that absolute truth exists regardless of whether we acknowledge it or not. Furthermore, objective truth is a reality regardless of our subjective opinion about it. Imagine a multi-car collision at a local intersection. Everyone involved in the accident has a different perspective on what happened. Bystanders also have their own interpretations of what occurred. Undoubtedly, some of the details of the various accounts will contradict one another depending upon how alert the witnesses were and their particular points-of-view. But everyone agrees on the main facts: a wreck happened, and several cars were involved.

Now the essential question is this: Does the fact that so many people's accounts differ mean that there is no truth about what happened? Through interviews and careful investigation, the police might be able to reconstruct within a high degree of probability what actually happened. But even if the police fail to do a thorough investigation, it does not mean there is no truth about the matter. But the philosophical relativist would argue that in fact there *is* no truth about the accident since everything is strictly a matter of opinion. But this is patently absurd. An accident actually occurred, and there are objective realities about how it happened which are true regardless of whether anyone fully realizes them or not.

The fact is that truth exists. It is not something we invent, but it *is* something we can discover. **Truth is objective – i.e., it is independent of our own subjective perceptions – and it is absolute, not relative. By definition: Truth is that which corresponds to reality**. As Aristotle explained it, "To say of what is, that it is not, or of what is not, that it is, is false; while to say of what is, that it is, and of what is not, that it is not, is true." So to say "There is no truth" is tantamount to declaring "There is no reality." But some things are objectively true even if they aren't obvious or generally accepted.

- Truth is reality – even if no one knows it.
- Truth is reality – even if no one admits it.
- Truth is reality – even if no one agrees what it is.
- Truth is reality – even if no one lives by it.
- Truth is true – even if no one but God understands it.

As the Quaker statesman William Penn once observed, "Right is right though all men be against it, and wrong is wrong though all be for it." Subjective opinions do not alter objective realities.

A Note on Relativism and Relational Comparisons
A Lesson From the Great American Pastime

Many things in life are "relative", but philosophical relativ*ism* is quite a different thing.

For example, if I were to say, "Nolan Ryan was a great Major League Baseball pitcher," I simply mean that he was far better than the average pitcher, and I can support my claim by citing his statistics that prove conclusively that he pitched more effectively over the course of his career than 99% of other pitchers.

But of course, there *is* an absolute standard of perfection for pitchers in which a pitcher throws a "perfect game" in every game he pitches (which means that he never allows a single hit, walk or run, and retires all 27 batters he faces in each game he pitches) – and by that standard Nolan Ryan was far from perfect. In fact, he never pitched a single perfect game in his entire career. But this standard is strictly theoretical and humanly unattainable, so realistically one can say that "relative" to other pitchers – or in terms of a relational comparison to other pitchers – Nolan Ryan truly was "great."

The key is to understand what the standard of comparison is. In this case, as with all physical realities, the standard is not absolute theoretical perfection but the Major League statistical average for pitchers. This is a purely human standard, and as the old sayings go, "Nobody's perfect" and "To err is human." (In this regard, baseball correlates to life in general: pitchers rarely pitch "perfect games," and players sometimes make errors.) But a baseball ignoramus may be oblivious to the fact that there are great pitcher," he might assume that this is merely my opinion rather than a truth-claim based on statistical data. In other words, he might assume that I mean, "Subjectively, I liked Nolan Ryan" rather than "Objectively, it is a fact that Nolan Ryan was a great pitcher."

There is a qualitative difference between this kind of relational comparison of temporal and physical realities and the philosophy of relativism that relates to eternal and transcendent realities. Philosophical relativism declares that there is no such thing as absolute truth nor any transcendent standards of measurement. On the contrary, the Bible asserts that absolute Truth exists and that the standard of perfection is the character and nature of God. As Einstein once commented, "Relativism relates [only] to the realm of physics, not ethics."

It is important that Christians keep this vital distinction in mind. Philosophical relativism denies the reality of absolute, eternal and transcendent Truth. Relational comparisons, on the other hand, simply apply to concepts that are human constructs or to things that are purely physical and temporal.

Therefore, a baseball is "big" compared to a golf ball but "small" compared to a basketball. The speed of a Nolan Ryan fastball was "fast" compared to how hard other human beings can throw (including virtually all other Major League pitchers) but "slow" compared to the velocity of a professional tennis player's serve. Everything in life that is physical and/or human in origin is relative in relation to (or by comparison to) other physical and/or human properties and products. But the philosophy of relativism is quite another thing: it is a skeptical rejection of all absolute, eternal, and transcendent Truth.

The Cultural Fault Line

The controversy regarding absolute truth is the critical fault line in the contemporary "culture war." As many of the old divisions between Protestants, Anabaptists, and Catholics and Orthodox Christians dissolve amid the wholesale assault on Christianity in the public square, a new spirit of cooperation is beginning to emerge. The battle lines in the culture war are usually depicted in political terms as a struggle between conservative versus liberal (or "progressive") socio/political ideologies, but in fact the divide is much deeper than politics and ideologies. Essentially, it is a chasm separating those who hold to traditional Biblically-based moral values and others who contend that truth and morality are relative, subjective, and merely a matter of personal preference.

Every day in America the culture war is waged in the workplace, in our schools, and even in many churches. It is total war, and it involves the whole spectrum of life issues from sexual morality to popular entertainment, business practices, the interpretation of current events, the curricula in local schools, sportsmanship in athletics, the development and application of certain technologies, and a myriad of other issues. In every venue of life there are those who seek to be guided by Biblically-derived principles that have been transmitted, however imperfectly, *via* our cultural heritage, and those who live their lives based exclusively on a subjective and relativistic moral code independent of any higher authority. The contrast between these two worldviews is often so sharp that historian Gertrude Himmelfarb likened it to two cultures existing within a single nation. Dennis Prager refers to it as a "cultural civil war." These two orientations are intrinsically contradictory, incompatible, and the source of most of the cultural, moral, and political dissonance that we observe in contemporary life. And unfortunately, as J. Budziszewski observes, the gulf separating these positions is growing wider than ever before.

> We are passing through an eerie phase of history in which the things that everyone really knows are treated as

unheard-of doctrines, a time in which the elements of common decency are themselves attacked as indecent. Nothing quite like this has ever happened before. Although our civilization has passed through quite a few troughs of immorality, never before has vice held the high *moral* ground. Our time considers it dirty-minded to treat sexual purity as a virtue... [and] a sign of impious pride to profess humble faith in God. The moral law has become the very emblem of immorality. We call affirming it "being judgmental" and "being intolerant"....

[But despite popular denial] the common moral truths are no less plain to us today than they ever have been.

[J. Budziszewski,, *What We Can't Not Know* (2003), pp. 10, 12.]

The tendency of many American Christians is to trace the origins of the culture war back to the 1960s, but in fact it did not begin with the Sexual Revolution, the emergence of radical feminism and LGBTQ activism, the abortion controversy, the rise of the counterculture, or any other *cause celebre* that emerged in those years. More fundamentally, the problem began with a relatively subtle intellectual paradigm shift in the 18th century that gradually replaced traditional sources of authority with the philosophy of **Enlightenment rationalism** – the belief that human reasoning alone is sufficient as a guide to truth and morality. In its rejection of special (divine) revelation, rationalism in turn set the stage in the following century for the emergence of **scientism** (or Logical Positivism, to use philosophical terminology) – the theory that the only objective realities in life are those that can be verified scientifically. As a naturalistic and materialistic philosophy, scientism undermines any basis for traditional Biblically-based morality, and the consequences can be devastating. History repeatedly confirms that what is intellectually respectable eventually becomes culturally acceptable, and as Charles Colson has commented, our current cultural crisis can be traced directly to the toxic effects of moral relativism and the rejection of an absolute moral standard. This is the insidious and divisive deception that is driving America's culture war and perpetuating the gridlock in our our political system. As Colson observed:

> How did we get into this mess?.... We dug the hole that became a cultural Grand Canyon when we abandoned belief in a moral truth that is knowable.
>
> People who reject transcendent authority can no longer persuade one another through rational arguments; everything is reduced to personal opinion. Debates about ideas thus degenerate into power struggles; we're left with no moral standard by which to measure the common good. For that matter, how can there be a "common good" without an objective standard for truth? The death of moral truth has fractured America into two warring camps.... This is why politics has become so ugly today.
> [Charles Colson, "The New Civil War." *Christianity Today* (Feb. 2003), p. 128]

From point of fact, relativism and subjectivism are nothing new. In classical Greece, philosophers who called themselves sophists (literally, "wise men") espoused the same kind of skeptical values that moral relativists embrace today. Sophists were subjectivists who believed that all knowledge comes via the five senses and is therefore limited to what an individual experiences. Therefore, they concluded, since no one experiences the full range of existential reality, we can never say for certain that anything *is* or *is not*. Sophists were also relativists who contended that there are no absolute standards of right and wrong, and they were humanists who considered individual self-fulfillment to be, ultimately, the only sensible and worthwhile goal in life. Their basic credo was neatly summarized by Protagoras' oft-quoted comment, "Man is the measure of all things." In other words, it is man, not the gods (or God – or any external universal moral code), that determines truth and morality. Everything is subjective and relative, and each person should live according to his own perceived self-interest.

Interestingly, it was opposition to sophism that motivated the great classical philosophers such as Socrates, Plato, and Aristotle to develop their moral philosophy. They knew full-well that relativism, subjectivism and humanistic individualism were a recipe for both personal and civic disaster. Nonetheless, the tenets of sophism hold great appeal to those intent on defining their own morality, and these concepts were transmitted through subsequent Hellenistic philosophies such as Skepticism, Epicureanism and Cynicism. Given the egoistic nature of humanity, it is not surprising that these values constantly resurface throughout history. In modern times, the philosophy of secular humanism based on materialism, rationalism and scientism revived these ancient sophist ideas and granted them renewed intellectual credibility in the context of a Western Civilization in wholesale rebellion against traditional Biblical Christian beliefs and practices.

Variations On the Theme

Relativism is absolutely pervasive in modern society and is manifest in a variety of ways.

Epistemological relativism holds that all knowledge is relative. In other words, we can know nothing for certain because our perception of the real world is dependent upon our own subjective mental constructs or those of our specific social group. Although the concept dates back to the sophists, in modern times it was revived and restated by Immanuel Kant in his influential work, *Critique of Pure Reason* (1781). According to Kant, concepts such as "objective reality" and "transcendent truth" are speculative and essentially meaningless. We can never know the reality of something in itself because everything is processed through the filter of our own subjective mind in accord with our own *a priori* assumptions and our unique life experiences. Therefore, everything is a matter of perspective and interpretation, and there is no way to see the world that is definitively "true."

Subsequent philosophers such as Friedrich Neitzsche (1844-1900) rejected the concept of objective truth altogether. For him, truth is unknowable because in fact truth does not exist. Or in other words, there is no truth – only opinions and assertions of truth. Of course, that was only his opinion, but in recent decades this kind of cynicism has become the basic premise of philosophical post-modernism. A classic expression of Orwellian "Newspeak," epistemological relativism redefines "truth" in strictly relativistic terms. Therefore, something can be "true" for one person but not for another, just as one person's "truth" may contradict another's "truth" and both be valid.

Today, many consider this notion to be quite tolerant and liberating since it makes every individual the final arbiter of right and wrong for him/herself. But in fact epistemological relativism is an unworkable and self-defeating premise since it reduces everything to subjective opinions and moral equivalencies, and thereby eliminates any bases for prudent discernment or sound judgment. But for those who prefer to be the masters of their own imaginary universe, epistemological relativism is the key to the kingdom.

Moral relativism rejects all moral and ethical absolutes and contends that nothing is necessarily right or wrong but solely dependent upon one's viewpoint and circumstances – or even one's preferences. This is, of course, a common and popular position of many, including for instance the science-fiction writer and radical libertarian Robert Heinlein, best-known for his novel, *Stranger in a Strange Land* (1961), who proudly declared:

> I am free, no matter what rules surround me. If I find them tolerable, I tolerate them; if I find them too obnoxious, I break them. I am free because I know that I alone am morally responsible for everything I do. [Quoted in Cal Thomas, "Rules? What Rules? http://townhall.com/columnists/cal thomas/2016/05/30/rules-what-rules-n2169609]

Like Heinlein, moral relativists are often astonishingly shallow thinkers, such as the atheist Michael Ruse who has written that morality is "merely an adaptation" that evolution "put in place to further our reproductive ends." Nonetheless, moral relativism is always a popular notion because it serves as a convenient rationalization for everything from narcissism, selfishness, and greed to unethical business practices, political corruption, racial discrimination, sexual exploitation, abortion-on-demand, and even genocide.

Religious relativism contends that all religions are man-made, and that no belief system is universally or exclusively true. This is the foundation for religious pluralism, which rejects the exclusive truth-claims of various religions (including, of course, the exclusive truth-claims of Jesus Christ) and attempts to argue that all religious paths are more-or-less equally valid (or invalid) and lead to the same destination. While it is true that many religions share some beliefs in common, in terms of their distinctive core doctrines – the nature of Ultimate Reality, the nature of humanity, humanity's basic problem, our purpose and meaning for existing, and our eternal destiny – the various religions offer drastically contrasting and irreconcilable interpretations and answers.

Cultural relativism, the philosophical basis for the obsession with "multiculturalism" and social "diversity" in American life, contends that there are no universal standards or principles by which to judge various cultures. Not only customs and mores, but also morality and ethics, vary from one culture to another, and all are more-or-less equally valid. Note: For the purpose of clarity, it is important to distinguish between the *sociology* of multiculturalism, which is simply the study of the unique characteristics of various societies and cultures, and the *ideology* of multiculturalism, which contends that various cultures are more-or-less qualitatively equal.

The cult of cultural relativism is a reaction to Western ethnocentrism in general and concepts such as American exceptionalism in particular. As with other forms of relativism, the ideology of multiculturalism is rather obviously absurd. If, for example, all cultures are equally valid, why, for the past four hundred years, have tens of millions of immigrants from all over the world left behind their native lands, families and cultural heritage to come, often at great risk, to America? Why not to Saudi Arabia or China or Mexico? What is it about the United States that is so attractive in contrast to Egypt, India or Kenya? And for those who would answer, "Well, of course, America is freer and richer than those other countries, and it offers more opportunities," we might ask, "Then *why* is America freer and *why* does it offer more opportunities than those other countries?" We certainly were not richer than many of them for the first 200 years of our existence. *Why* did America become the most free and prosperous nation in human history? Is there not something unique about its cultural heritage that sets it apart? And if so, then the arguments for cultural relativism collapse under the weight of historical realities.

Historical relativism, as argued by postmodernists, maintains that there is no objective truth when it comes to interpretations of the past. Everything is subjective and depends upon the particular values and points-of-view of historians themselves. As above, a corollary to this notion is that no historian's particular interpretation is necessarily more valid than another's. But as with all scholarship, we know that while no historian is infallible, some are indisputably more knowledgeable, more objective, more fair and more honest than others.

So while it is true that history is a narrative art form that incorporates personal and subjective components in terms of the researching and writing of the past, nonetheless there are historical realities that are undeniably objective. Certain things actually did happen in a particular time and place and were themselves the results of specific causes that produced certain effects. Given a sound mind, the requisite level of knowledge, and adequate source materials, competent and honest historians can in fact reconstruct and interpret the past with reasonable accuracy. This is not impossible, and in fact it happens quite regularly. Furthermore, as the Polish philosopher and historian Leszek Kolakowski has written, historical relativism not only defies reason and reality, but it constitutes a dishonest attempt to evade moral responsibility.

> Saying that "there are no facts, only interpretations" has another, dangerous meaning. Since historical knowledge is supposed to consist in the description of facts, of things that really happened, the idea that there are no facts in the normal sense implies that interpretations do not depend on facts but the other way around: that facts are produced by interpretations.... In other words, the concept of a moral judgment, and therefore also the concepts of good and evil, are empty; they do not refer to any empirical reality but only to our way of judging reality according to our *a priori* conceptual framework that we have constructed.
>
> The doctrine that "there are no facts; there are only interpretations" abolishes the idea of human responsibility and moral judgments; in effect, it considers any myth, legend, or fable just as valid, in terms of knowledge, as any fact that we have verified as such according to our standards of historical inquiry. In epistemological terms, any mythical story is just as good as any historically established fact; the story of Hercules fighting against the Hydra is no worse – no less true – in historical terms, than the history of Napoleon's defeat at Waterloo. There are no valid rules for establishing truth; consequently, there is no such thing as truth.
>
> There is no need to elaborate on the disastrous cultural effects of such a theory. [Leszek Kolakowski, 5 Nov 2003, acceptance speech for the John W. Kluge Prize Lifetime Achievement Award in the Human Sciences, November 5, 2003.]

Aesthetic relativism is the view that beauty is purely relative to different individuals and/or cultures. As with other forms of philosophical relativism, this concept was first articulated in ancient Greece and is often expressed in Protagoras' declaration, "Beauty is in the eye of the beholder." In other words, everything is subjective. There are no aesthetic standards for art – including literature, music, architecture, the performing arts or the visual arts – and one person's opinion is as valid as another's. So presumably, Handel's "Messiah" has no more qualitative artistic value than the latest outpouring of verbal diarrhea from some rancid gangsta rapper. But anyone today who would argue that some music, some literature or some films are better than others had best be prepared to defend his/her assertion against the common mindless rebuttal, "But that's just your opinion!"

The Tyranny of Relativism

Although relativism is often defended on the basis of "tolerance", there is a tyrannical side to relativism that is often unacknowledged. From the preceding, it is obvious that relativism is a serious hindrance to the search for truth, which is an innate and irrepressible human desire. Whether we realize it or not, we instinctively pursue truth because we inherently and intuitively value reality. But philosophical relativism denies that anything is objectively true or objectively knowable. As we have discussed, this is fundamentally incoherent and counterintuitive, and no one can live consistently in accord with such a philosophy.

Relativism regards all judgment and discrimination between alternatives as bigoted prejudice. Likewise, all argument and persuasion are dismissed not as means toward the greater goal of achieving true understanding but as merely tactical power plays by those seeking to dominate and manipulate others. When applied to the realm of religious faith, relativism asserts that everyone has a right to believe whatever he/she prefers, and any kind of rational and fact-based argumentation is tantamount to "forcing your religion on others" and a violation of another's free will.

For relativists, those who profess to believe in absolute and exclusive truth are automatically characterized as arrogant, narrow-minded, dogmatic, insensitive, and intolerant bigots. Never mind that the believer's arguments may be valid and true, because relativists are convinced that ultimately nothing is universally valid and true except the premise that nothing is universally valid and true. In a postmodern culture in which relativism often goes unchallenged, the premier virtue then becomes "**tolerance**". But this is a selective kind of tolerance, of course, because it is absolutely intolerant of those who believe in absolute truth. Purporting to celebrate tolerance and diversity, relativists seek to impose uniformity of thought and belief based on their personal ideology while refusing to tolerate any contrary beliefs that challenge their relativistic assumptions. **The irony is that those who promote tolerance and diversity most vociferously tend to be most intolerant of those who challenge the absolutism of tolerance and diversity.**

Furthermore, relativists fail even to understand what tolerance really means. As the term is often used today, it usually connotes a totally non-discriminating acceptance of anything and everything. **But in fact, true tolerance acknowledges the fundamental reality that some beliefs or practices are fallacious, immoral or inferior while also acknowledging that those who believe or practice such things should not be harassed, discriminated against or persecuted because of their beliefs and practices. In other words, tolerance is not agreement or acceptance. Therefore, rather than being an argument for relativism, tolerance actually implies just the opposite.**

Similarly, relativists misunderstand the value of open-mindedness. As Allan Bloom observed, "Openness used to be the virtue that permitted us to seek the good by using reason. It now means accepting everything and denying reason's power." So in effect open-mindedness becomes little more than empty-headedness. It accepts everything uncritically while requiring no evidence or no rationale. In reducing everything to subjective personal opinion, it contributes to the mindless anti-intellectualism of our day. No wonder, as philosopher Larry Laudan notes in *Science and Relativism*, so many people are so easily misled and manipulated by media bias and political propaganda.

> The displacement of the idea that facts and evidence matter by the idea that everything boils down to subjective interests and perspectives is – second only to American political campaigns – the most prominent and pernicious manifestation of anti-intellectualism in our time. [Larry Laudan, *Science and Relativism: Some Key Controversies in the Philosophy of Science* (1990), p. 27.]

The intellectual and moral consequences of relativism can be frightening. One of its worst effects is that it renders all education meaningless. If relativism is true and nothing can be known for certain, we can never really learn anything since the process of learning involves progressing from ignorance to enlightenment – or from false notions to true understanding. As a result, an education system based on relativistic principles relegates itself to irrelevancy. This intellectual conundrum has become apparent in many fields of the social sciences and humanities where scholars and teachers have been sucked into the black hole of postmodern relativism to the point that their own academic discipline is discredited and rendered meaningless. The end result is abject nihilism, such as that expressed by postmodern historians who argue that the real lesson of history is that we can learn virtually nothing from history. For such cynics, the only apparent value of history is that it provides jobs for historians who believe there is no value in history.

Another destructive consequence of relativism is its corrosive effect on the integrity and credibility of language. Those who believe in truth strive to communicate their understanding of it as clearly and precisely as possible. But as pastor and theologian John Piper observes, "When objective truth vanishes in the fog of relativism, the role of language changes dramatically." Language no longer seeks to convey truth, and it cuts itself loose from any objective external reality. Instead, it manufactures a purely subjective and relativistic reality of its own and becomes merely an expression of power and manipulation.

When language is relativized, the goal no longer is the honest communication of reality but the manipulation of reality. Words and terms degenerate into mere semantics, and propaganda rather than truth prevails. A century ago, the theologian John Gresham Machen observed the re-emergence of relativism as a dominant philosophical trend and warned of its purely "utilitarian view of language." According to Machen, relativism is intrinsically dishonest in its cavalier treatment of language, and he saw it as an indispensable tool for those whose goal is to confuse, mislead and exploit others. Subsequently, even secular social critics such as George Orwell and Aldous Huxley warned of the potential damage of the perversion of language in their dystopian novels *Animal Farm*, *Nineteen Eighty-Four* and *Brave New World*.

In his astute social critique, *The Technological Society*, the French social scientist Jacques Ellul noted that two features of modern culture have contributed more than all others to the corruption of language: political propaganda and commercial advertising – both of which show utter disregard for the integrity of words. But Ellul was writing in the 1950s and '60s – prior to the advent of "political-correctness" and the emergence of postmodernism as a dominant intellectual trend – so he could hardly imagine the ultimate degradation of language by those who cynically exploit it in education, politics, the media and pop culture for its pragmatic and propagandistic value.

The ultimate consequences of relativism can be catastrophic. As Nietzsche observed in *The Antichrist* (1888), in the absence of truth, power prevails. In other words, if there is no acknowledged higher standard by which we measure and compare conflicting beliefs, the only resolution is a power struggle in which the strongest or the shrewdest prevails. Therefore, in his declaration concerning the "death of God" and the collapse of any objective standard of truth and morality, Nietzsche predicted a century marked by cynicism and nihilistic despair. With the loss of meaning and hope, chaos would fill the vacuum and prepare the way for the total breakdown of the individual as well as society, culture, and civilization itself. But history shows that social and political chaos create only a temporary power vacuum, and what often follows is the reimposition of law and order via some form of tyranny. In Nietsche's Germany, of course, the particular form of tyranny that eventually emerged was Nazi totalitarianism.

Today, we are well on our way down the path to total social and cultural breakdown. When relativism prevails, people lose their moral bearings and, as in the days of Noah, begin to define right and wrong individualistically. When such a trend reaches a critical mass, all personal and societal standards collapse. Prior to his election as Pope Benedict XVI in 2005, Cardinal Joseph Ratzinger warned that"We are moving towards a dictatorship of relativism which does not recognize anything as certain, and which has as its highest goal one's own ego and one's own desires." In such a scenario, people lose sight of any common good and everything degenerates into a chaotic nightmare of competitive power plays in which individuals and special interest groups scheme and maneuver to advance their agendas. As anarchy engulfs society and the entire cultural house of cards collapses, the end result is what the French social scientist Jean Francois Revel referred to as "the totalitarian temptation" – a crisis so threatening that the masses surrender all sovereignty to an authoritarian government in exchange for peace and security. John Piper describes the scenario this way:

> When the chaos of relativism reaches a certain point, the people will welcome any ruler who can bring some semblance of order and security. So a dictator [or a

political party] steps forward and crushes the chaos with absolute control. Ironically, relativism – the great lover of unfettered freedom – destroys freedom in the end. [John Piper, "The Challenge of Relativism." An address to the Ligonier National Conference, March 16, 2007.]

This is the ultimate triumph of relativistic Social Darwinism – and as Charles Colson has noted, Political Darwinism: an amoral survival of the fittest – or the triumph of the shrewdest and the most ruthless in which might makes right and morality and ethics are rendered irrelevant.

Relativism and Logic

Relativism is insidious because it undermines morality, and it is untrue because it contradicts reality. Harold Pinter, a Nobel Prize winner in Literature for 2005, is a typical product of postmodern philosophical confusion. On the one hand he declares with absolute certainty that "there is no hard distinctions between what is real and what is unreal, nor between what is true and what is false." Furthermore, nothing is "necessarily true or false; it can be both true *and* false."

Yet when it comes to American foreign relations, Pinter thinks he has no problem distinguishing between truth and falsehood. For instance, he is quite certain that virtually everything the United States does in the world is bad and most everything its critics charge is true. People like Pinter exemplify the need to restore a substantive core curriculum in the liberal arts and humanities in our high schools and universities. He should never have been allowed to graduate from high school (or a university) without first passing an introductory course in Philosophy 101: Logic and Critical Thinking and demonstrating functional competency in the basic laws of logic – including the following principles.*

---

* For a useful introduction to the principles of logic and critical thinking, see Norman L. Geisler and Ronald M. Brooks, *Come Let Us Reason: An Introduction to Logical Thinking* (Baker Book House, 1990).

The Law of Identity. Many things in life are self-evident and incontestable (except perhaps to lunatics, people tripping on LSD, and a few oddball intellectuals with advanced degrees in critical race and gender studies). Of all the self-evident principles of logic, the most elementary is the Law of Identity. This is about as basic as things get, and Aristotle summarized it this way: "To say of what is that it is, or what is not that it is not, is true."

Simply stated, the Law of Identity ("**A is A**") declares that something is identical to itself and different from other things – regardless of their similarities or dissimilarities. In other words, if something is 'A' then it is 'A' – not 'non-A' or 'B' or 'C'. Furthermore, if something exists then it is ontologically real. This is true for molecules, for stars, for snowflakes, for organisms, for human beings, for words, for numbers, and for truth claims.

The Law of Non-Contradiction. Logically, relativism is rather obviously fallacious. Statements such as "There is no absolute truth" and "Everything is relative" are innately self-contradictory because they are themselves absolute statements of fact – or absolute truth statements. According to the Law of Non-Contradiction ("**A is not non-A**"), if something is self-contradictory it is illogical and therefore untrue. Something cannot be both 'A' and 'non-A' in the same sense, at the same time, or in the same relation. If opposites could be true, there would be no difference between truth and falsehood or between reality and non-reality.

The Law of the Excluded Middle. The Law of the Excluded Middle makes the obvious observation that "**Either something is A or non-A.**" It is a simple either/or proposition, and there are no other options. Something either exists or it does not exist; a statement is either true or untrue. But relativism regularly embraces contradictory propositions, and therefore it violates this law and fails the truth test (not to mention the straight-face test).

These and similar laws of logic demonstrate that truth and reality are inescapable. Those who deny objective truth are asserting an objective truth in the sense that relativism claims to be absolutely (and objectively) true for everyone. Hence, it is self-contradictory, illogical, and nonsensical. Even worse, relativism is a fundamental deception and the philosophical foundation for much of the muddled thinking and dysfunctional living that is common today. Christians who take their faith seriously should be aware of just how pervasive and pernicious relativism is, and how it corrodes any faith and confidence in the truth claims of the Bible and the historic Christian faith.

The Self-Excepting Fallacy. When postmodern relativists such as Harold Pinter utter absolute truth statements such as, "There is no absolute truth," they obviously would like us to believe the same thing they believe. Essentially, they are making an absolute claim that relativism is absolutely true and absolutism is absolutely false. But if, as Pinter asserts, nothing is "necessarily either true or false," why should we accept his statement as true or pay any attention whatsoever to it?

For his statement to have any validity, the relativist would have to say, "Nothing is objectively true – including my own relativistic assertion." But of course an admission like this would render his statement meaningless and seriously undermine his authority and influence. Furthermore, if it were true that something could be "true for you, but not for me," then why would I take it seriously or think that it applies to me?

The relativist, in claiming that his statements about relativism are true for everyone except himself, commits the Self-Excepting Fallacy. He holds that everything is relative except his own view of relativism, which he regards as absolute. But logically we cannot say, "Nothing is universally true," and then turn around and declare, "My view is universally true." In real life, the only people who usually get away with such inane absurdities are the talking heads on television, tenured faculty, and Democratic politicians.

An Analysis of Moral Relativism

In contemporary culture, tolerance has been elevated to the status of the ultimate value, and people have been taught to believe that the mortal enemy of tolerance is belief in absolute, objective truth. In fact, tolerance may be virtually the only value on which there is a postmodernist consensus, as Allan Bloom relates in *The Closing of the American Mind*:

> The danger [we] have been taught to fear from absolutism is not error, but intolerance. Relativism is necessary to openness; and this is the virtue, the only virtue, which all primary education for more than 50 years has dedicated itself to inculcating. The true believer is the real danger.
> [Allan Bloom, *The Closing of the American Mind* (1987), p. 25]

But in fact, relativism is an indefensible illusion. Although many people are selectively relativistic, no one is consistently relativistic. Like everyone else, relativists usually behave as if they believe that certain concepts and behaviors are objectively right and wrong. When they are personally offended or their rights are violated, they recognize the injustice of it all and respond as anyone else would. Their innate moral sensibilities contradict their relativistic assertions because in order to deny an absolute, one must make an absolute denial. Furthermore, how could anyone be absolutely certain that there are no absolutes unless they were absolutely omniscient?

In his most famous work, *Mere Christianity*, C. S. Lewis builds a systematic case for the coherence of the Christian faith by first establishing the existence of moral absolutes, or what moral philosophers traditionally have referred to as **Natural Law**. Lewis argues that there is a universal moral law, which he calls the "Law of Human Nature," that functions as a commonly-held standard of right and wrong. Because we are made in the image of a God who is the essence and the personification of all goodness, we have a sense of this moral law although none of us keeps it consistently. Lewis contends that these two facts – our innate awareness of the moral law and the fact that we regularly violate it – are "the foundation of all clear thinking about ourselves and the universe we live in."*

Some argue that our sense of morality is culturally-induced, and that if we lived in a different culture we would have drastically different values. There is no doubt that our culture and our life experiences *condition* our values and beliefs, but they do not *determine* who and what we are. Every individual is morally accountable and has a degree of free will, and no one is completely a helpless pawn or a hapless victim of their society and its values. Otherwise, how do we explain the existence of those in virtually every society who are nonconformists, independent thinkers, and who hold radically different countercultural values and beliefs – including many Christians throughout the centuries?

Although cultural diversity is certainly a fact, it does not follow that moral relativism is a fact. Some cultures are simply more enlightened than others, and some have a richer moral and ethical tradition. For example, from its founding America was influenced in part by Biblical Christian values, so it should not be surprising or coincidental that our moral and ethical traditions have been relatively enlightened *vis-a-vis* most other cultures. (Note: Of course, this does not ignore other cultural influences in early American history such as Enlightenment rationalism and classical liberal political philosophy, nor does it imply that Biblically-based values have been actualized consistently throughout our history.)

Furthermore, different cultures do in fact generally agree on fundamental principles of right and wrong. All societies have a sense of certain inviolable moral and ethical standards dealing with concepts such as honor, justice, and propriety. The manner in which these standards are practiced often differ from one culture to another, but cultures generally agree on the basic moral principles

---

* For an extended treatment of the history and philosophy of natural moral law, see chapter 2 in Jefrey D. Breshears, *American Crisis: Cultural Marxism and the Culture War – A Christian Response* (Centre•Pointe Publishing, 2020).

of Natural Law even if the applications (and perhaps the definitions) vary. And of course, the applications differ simply because, once again, some cultures are more enlightened than others, and some have a richer moral and ethical tradition than others. Just as there are no two people who are truly equal, likewise no two cultures are equal despite the propaganda put forth by multiculturalist ideologues.

In his essay, "The Poison of Subjectivism," C. S. Lewis dismissed the multiculturalist argument for moral relativism as a "resounding lie" while upholding the validity of a universal and transcultural moral code based on Natural Law principles.

> If a man will go into a library and spend a few days with the *Encyclopedia of Religion and Ethics* he will soon discover the massive unanimity of the practical reason of man. From [the perusal of various ancient religious texts] he will collect the same triumphantly monotonous denunciations of oppression, murder, treachery, and falsehood, the same injunctions of kindness to the aged, the young, and the weak, of alms- giving and impartiality and honesty.... [H]e will no longer doubt that there is such a thing as the Law of Nature. There are, of course, differences. There are even blindnesses in particular cultures.... But the pretence that we are presented with a mere chaos – in which no outline of universally accepted value shows through – is wherever it is simply false and should be contradicted.... Far from finding a chaos, we find exactly what we should expect if good is indeed something objective and reason the organ whereby it is apprehended – that is, a substantial agreement with considerable local differences of emphasis and, perhaps, no one code that includes everything. [C. S. Lewis, "The Poison of Subjectivism." http://wwwcalvinedupribeiroblogspot.com/2009/01/poison-of-subjectivism.html]

Some challenge the concept of a universal moral law by attributing it to naturalistic factors. For them, what we erroneously assume to be a divinely-endowed sense of right and wrong is just simple human impulses. For philosophical naturalists, everything is reducible to materialistic factors – everything from our DNA to the moral standards of our society. They contend that morality has nothing to do with the fact that we have an innate spiritual nature; perhaps we simply have some kind of yet-to-be-discovered "moral gene" or "God particle" embedded in our physiology.

But there is a problem with the naturalistic explanation. **Natural impulses are simply desires, whereas the moral law is a mandate. It doesn't tell us what we *feel* like doing but what we *ought* to do.** If it were self-imposed, we could unilaterally liberate ourselves from it and its demands. But in fact we cannot. According to Lewis, this mandate is an objective standard by which we measure alternative options – and as an example he cited our response when we hear an urgent cry for help. Immediately, we experience two impulses: (1) rescue the victim; and (2) avoid getting hurt ourselves – the self-preservation instinct. Now, regardless of how strong the latter impulse may be, we feel as though we *should* intervene. As Lewis explained, "Now this thing that judges between two instincts, that decides which should be encouraged, cannot itself be either of them." It must come from without the individual, not within.

In fact, any suggestion that something may be right or wrong points to a universal standard. If relativism were true, there would have to be something to which all things are relative but which is not itself relative. In other words, something ultimately has to be absolute before we can see that something else is relative to it. Therefore, there must be something which does not change by which we can measure the variations in everything else. In *Mere Christianity* Lewis summarizes the argument this way:

> The moment you say that one set of moral ideas can be better than another, you are measuring them both by a standard, saying that one of them conforms to that standard more nearly than the other. But the standard

that measures two things is something different from either. You are, in fact, comparing them both with some Real Morality, admitting that there is such a thing as a real Right, independent of what people think. [C. S. Lewis, *Mere Christianity* (1952), p. 13.]

In the first two chapters of his epistle to the Romans, the apostle Paul sets forth the case for Natural Law. In this passage, he argues that an awareness of the innate moral law is both universal and inescapable. This divinely-implanted sense of morality is clearly revealed in nature just as it is inherent to basic human nature.

> I am not ashamed of the gospel, because it is the power of God for the salvation of everyone who believes... For in the gospel a righteousness from God is revealed....
>
> The wrath of God is being revealed from heaven against all the godlessness and wickedness of men who suppress the truth by their wickedness, since what may be known about God is plain to them, because God has made it plain to them. For since the creation of the world God's invisible qualities – his eternal power and divine nature – have been clearly seen, being understood from what has been made, so that men are without excuse.
>
> For although they knew [about] God, they neither glorified him as God nor gave thanks to him, but their thinking became futile and their foolish hearts were darkened. Although they claimed to be wise, they became fools and exchanged the glory of the immortal God for [various idols]....
>
> Therefore God gave them over in the sinful desires of their hearts to sexual impurity for the degrading of their bodies with one another. They exchanged the truth of God for a lie, and worshiped and served created things rather than the Creator....
>
> Because of this God gave them over to shameful lusts [culminating in homosexuality]....
>
> Furthermore, since they did not think it worthwhile to retain the knowledge of God, he gave them over to a

depraved mind, to do what ought not to be done. They have become filled with every kind of wickedness, evil, greed, and depravity. They are full of envy, murder, strife, deceit and malice. They are gossips, slanderers, God-haters, insolent, arrogant and boastful; they invent ways of doing evil;... they are senseless, faithless, heartless, ruthless. Although they know God's righteous decree that those who do such things deserve death, they not only continue to do these very things but also approve of those who practice them....

Because of your stubbornness and your unrepentant heart, you are storing up wrath against yourself for the day of God's wrath, when his righteous judgment will be revealed. God "will give to each person according to what he has done" [Psalm 62:12]. To those who by persistence in doing good seek glory, honor and immortality, he will give eternal life. But for those who are self-seeking and who reject the truth and follow evil, there will be wrath and anger. There will be trouble and distress for every person who does evil... but glory, honor and peace for everyone who does good.... God does not show favoritism.

All [non-Jews] who sin [out of ignorance of the Mosaic Law] will... perish apart from the law, and all [Jews] who sin under the [Mosaic Law] will be judged by the law. For it is not those who hear the [Mosaic Law] who are righteous in God's sight, but it is those who obey the law who will be declared righteous. Indeed, when non-Jews, who do not have the [Mosaic Law], do by nature things required by the law, they are a law for themselves, even though they do not have the [Mosaic Law], since they show that the requirement of [God's moral law] are written on their hearts, their consciences also bearing witness, and their thoughts now accusing, now even defending them. – Romans 1:16*ff*

Despite the tendency of many to deny it, these common moral truths that Paul alludes to in Romans 1-2 are every bit as apparent to us today as they always have been. They are applicable to all humanity, and at some level they are perceived by everyone. J. Budziszewski calls this innate moral consciousness "what we can't not know" – i.e., it is a kind of "universal common sense of the human race" that is "built into the design of human nature and woven into the fabric of the normal human mind."

Christians realize that the source of Natural Law is God himself, and it is inherent to human nature because we have been created in the *imago Dei* – the image of God. In his classic, *The Pursuit of God*, A. W. Tozer comments on the divine nature of this reality.

> There must be somewhere a fixed center against which everything else is measured, where the law of relativity does not enter, and we can say "IS" and make no allowances. Such a center is God. [A. W. Tozer, *The Pursuit of God* (1948), p.94.]

Tozer proceeds to explain that when God revealed his name to Moses as "I AM," God was implying that his essence and nature is the sovereign, infinite, and immutable absolute for all that exists, and that "Everyone and everything else measures from that fixed point."

There are, of course, those who seem appallingly oblivious to right and wrong. These are people who appear to kill, rape, steal, defraud, and exploit others unconscionably. Such people certainly seem incapable of distinguishing right and wrong – or at least they appear incapable of choosing right over wrong. Some are mentally ill and have been so severely damaged psychologically that they are functionally incapable of thinking morally. Others, through conscious and persistent bad choices, have violated their consciences to the point that their pathology has become habitual. In some cases, there are those who have even opened themselves up to demonic influences. And of course many people have develop debilitating chemical addictions, living perpetually in a drug- or alcohol-induced stupor, their will power and self-esteem so devastated as to render them morally impotent. But no sane and sober person can fail to distinguish between obvious right and wrong. Any normal person can see a qualitative difference between a Mahatma Gandhi and an Adolf Hitler, or between a Mother Theresa and a Lady Gaga.

In summation: Philosophical relativism is illogical, immature, impractical, intellectually and morally bankrupt, and the greatest single impediment to an honest search for truth, meaning and purpose in life. It is, in effect, the foundational deception of our time.

The Ultimate Virtue

If relativists are wrong and tolerance is not the ultimate virtue in life, what is? Or is anything at all? In fact, the Bible is quite clear on the matter. Although there is a hierarchy of virtues, there is one that is supreme and never dependent upon situations, conditions or circumstances. To quote the apostle Paul in I Corinthians 13:13, "the greatest of these is love." It is the ultimate moral virtue.

The key, of course, is love *as properly understood*. Of all the words and concepts that have been perverted through the ages, perhaps none has been so misunderstood and misapplied as the kind of love Paul refers to in I Corinthians 13. He uses the Greek word, ***agape***, which had a well-defined and specific meaning. The connotation that best describes *agape* is when we speak of "selfless" or "sacrificial" love – i.e., love with no strings attached that emanates from pure motives and no hidden agenda.

A good working definition of *agape* is that put forth by the psychiatrist, Scott Peck, in his book, *The Road Less Traveled*: **"Love is the will to extend oneself for the purpose of nurturing one's own or another person's spiritual growth."** In other words, love is far more than a sentiment, and it goes beyond mere emotion. Love is the commitment to do what is essential for one's own or another person's spiritual development. This is a wholistic definition that incorporates three elements: (1) intentionality (or motive); (2) actions (or will); and (3) a specific goal (or purpose).

Peck's definition is also satisfyingly wholistic in the sense that if we are to nurture our own or another's "spiritual growth," we understand that we must attend to the total person – including the physical, material, intellectual, psychological, social, and creative aspects of one's being. This is what Jesus inferred when he imparted the Golden Rule – "Do unto others as you would have them do unto you" – and when he proclaimed the Greatest Commandment: "Love the Lord God with all your heart, soul, mind, and strength, and love others as you love yourself."

Many prominent philosophers have recognized this reality and made it a foundational component of their philosophical system. For Immanuel Kant, all moral principles could be reduced to one central absolute – what he called the Categorical Imperative: "Would I want this action to be a universal practice of all people?" and "Would I want this action to be practiced on me?" For Martin Buber it was the "I-Thou" principle: We treat others not as "Its" – objects to be used – but as "Thous" – persons created in the image of God and worthy of respect. According to Buber, when we put this principle into action, it eventually leads us to a spiritual and metaphysical reality beyond ourselves and others. As he conceptualized it, "Extended, the lines of relationships intersect in the Eternal You."

The greatest way we can love another is to care for their soul as we do their physical well-being. We do this through sharing the truth in a spirit of love, including the truth of God's love through belief in Jesus Christ and the path to spiritual wholeness *via* Christian discipleship. This kind of love transcends mere tolerance, just as it incorporates all other values and virtues. If we truly believe Jesus' words when he declared, "I am the Way, the Truth, and the Life; no one comes to God the Father except through me," then the greatest act of love we can show to another is to share our faith in the One who testified before Pontius Pilate: "It is for this reason that I came into the world, to testify to the Truth" (John 18:37).

A Matter of Motives

One might reasonably ask, "If moral relativism is so transparently illogical and unrealistic, why do so many people – including many intelligent people – embrace it?" In most cases, the reason seems to be quite simple: As human beings with a sinful (i.e., self-centered) nature, we are capable of rationalizing most anything that we perceive to be to our advantage. Moral relativism feeds our egos and our passions by denying that any authority is over and above our own mind and will. With moral relativism, we can be the captain of our own soul – or perhaps even become our own god. This was, of course, the original lie that prompted the seminal sin that led to the Fall of mankind (Gen. 3:4-5).

Furthermore, if moral relativism is right, nothing is innately wrong. Therefore, we are not accountable to any Higher Power or any moral law above and beyond our own preferences. As the 17th century French philosopher Blaise Pascal commented, "People almost invariably arrive at their beliefs not on the basis of proof but on the basis of what they find attractive." Likewise, the singer/songwriter Paul Simon echoed this sentiment in his popular song, "The Boxer," when he wrote: "Still a man hears what he wants to hear / And disregards the rest."

Occasionally, relativists are surprisingly candid about their lack of interest in God and morality. Consider these admissions by notable skeptics:

- The renowned atheist and evolutionist, Sir Julian Huxley, admitted in *Essays of a Humanist*: "The sense of spiritual relief which comes from rejecting the idea of God as a supernatural being is enormous." [*Essays of a Humanist* (Pelican/ Penguin Books, 1966), p. 223.]

- Friedrich Nietsche in *The Antichrist* (1887): "It is our *preference* that decides against Christianity, not arguments." [Friedrich Nietzsche, *The AntiChrist*. Quoted in Os Guinness, *Time for Truth* (BakerBooks, 2000), p. 114.]
- Steven Weinberg, a Nobel laureate in physics: "Most scientists I know don't care enough about religion even to call themselves atheists." [Quoted in Natalie Angier, "Confessions of a Lonely Atheist," *The New York Times*, Jan. 14, 2001.)
- Sci-fi writer Isaac Asimov: "Emotionally I am an atheist. I don't have the evidence to prove that God doesn't exist, but I so strongly suspect he doesn't that I don't want to waste my time." [Cited in Ron Rhodes, *Answering the Objections of Atheists, Agnostics and Skeptics* (Harvest House Publishers, 2006), p. 21.]
- NYU philosopher Thomas Nagel: "I want atheism to be true and am made uneasy by the fact that some of the most intelligent and well-informed people I know are religious believers. It isn't just that I don't believe in God and, naturally, hope that I'm right in my belief. It's that I hope there is no God! I don't want there to be a God; I don't want the universe to be like that." [Thomas Nagel, *The Last Word* (Oxford University Press, 1997), p. 130]
- Aldous Huxley, a cousin of Julian Huxley, candidly admitted that the reason he and most of his colleagues eagerly embraced moral relativism was because belief in God and moral absolutes restricted their sexual options: "I had motives for not wanting the world to have meaning, consequently assumed that it had none, and was able without any difficulty to find satisfying reasons for this assumption.... For myself  [and my associates], the philosophy of meaninglessness was essentially an instrument of liberation. The liberation we desired was simultaneously liberation from a certain political and economic system and liberation from a

certain system of morality. We objected to the morality because it interfered with our sexual freedom." [Aldous Huxley, *Ends and Means: An Inquiry Into the Nature of Ideals and Into the Methods Employed for Their Realization* (Greenwood Publishing, 1969), pp. 270, 273.]

So much for the myth that religious skeptics are great thinkers who are simply too learned and wise to accept the arguments for the Christian faith. As is clear from these comments, the roadblock is usually a moral problem, not an intellectual issue. After all, as Dostoevsky noted in *The Brothers Karamazov*, if there is no God, then everything is permissible. Dinesh D'Souza puts it this way in *What's So Great About Christianity*: "If God does not exist, the seven deadly sins are not terrors to be overcome but temptations to be enjoyed." D'Souza proceeds to summarize the major problem with moral relativism and religious skepticism:

> My conclusion is that contrary to popular belief, atheism is not primarily an intellectual revolt, it is a moral revolt. Atheists don't find God invisible so much as objectionable .... The atheist seeks to get rid of moral judgment by getting rid of the judge. [Dinesh D'Souza, *What's So Great About Christianity* (2007), p. 272.]

Blaise Pascal regarded such skepticism as not only unreasonable, immature and irresponsible, but utterly insane. Since knowledge of the divine is the most important thing in life, any reasonable individual should make it his number one priority. Instead, many avoid not only the reality of God but the inevitability of death, and spend their precious time and energy pursuing all the things in life that are ultimately meaningless: wealth, power, status, success, and pleasure. As for what really matters, many refuse to be bothered. In his notes on apologetics, the *Pensees*, Pascal expressed the sentiments of the mass of humanity:

> I know not who sent me into the world, nor what the world is, nor what I myself am. I am terribly ignorant of everything. I know not what my body is, nor my senses, nor my soul, [nor my mind]....

The Absolute Truth About Relativism

> I see the terrifying immensity of the universe which surrounds me, and find myself limited to one corner of this vast expanse, without knowing why I am set down here... nor why the brief period appointed for my life is assigned to me at this moment rather than another in all the eternity that has gone before and will come after me. On all sides I behold nothing but infinity, in which I am... a mere passing shadow that returns no more. All I know is that I must soon die, but what I understand least of all is this very death which I cannot escape.
>
>
>
> As I know not whence I come, so I know not whither I go. I only know that on leaving this world I fall forever into nothingness or into the hands of a wrathful God, without knowing to which of these two states I shall be everlastingly consigned. Such is my condition, full of weakness and uncertainty. From all this I conclude that I ought to spend every day of my life seeking to know my fate. I might perhaps be able to find a solution to my doubts; but I cannot be bothered to do so, nor will I take one step towards its discovery. And after treating with contempt those who are concerned about such matters, I will go without foresight... and let myself drift toward death, uncertain of the eternity of my future state. [Blaise Pascal, *Pensees* 194.]

This is the condition of those without God: adrift in their own little life raft on the river of life, they are swept toward their own existential Niagara Falls with no sense of why they are here or their ultimate destiny. This is the fate of those who lack the courage to face reality. This is also the absolute truth about relativism.

Notes

Questions for Reflection and Discussion

1. In summary, what do you consider to be the thesis of this chapter?
2. The Christian philosopher Peter Kreeft has written that of all the symptoms of decay in our decadent culture, relativism is the most disastrous. Do you agree or not – and why?
3. Consider the statement on page 41: "What good does it do to proclaim that 'Jesus Christ is the Way, the Truth and the Life' if people reject the whole concept of objective truth?" How would an understanding of this principle change the way most Christians try to share their faith?
4. How have relativism and subjectivism corrupted people's sensitivities and sensibilities regarding how they view the arts and entertainment?
5. How does relativism relate to religious pluralism?
6. Complete this sentence: "Ultimately, the only reason for being a Christian is if in fact the Christian faith is _____ ."
7. Simply stated, what is truth?
8. Explain the difference between philosophical relativism and the kinds of relational comparisons that we commonly make in everyday life.
9. What are the intellectual and moral consequences of relativism?
10. What is the real meaning of "tolerance" and "open-mindedness?" Are tolerance and open-mindedness absolute virtues or conditional (or situational) values? Why?

11. What is the concept of Natural Law, and why is it the foundation for social and political civility?

12. In what ways is philosophical relativism the foundational deception of our time?

13. Define the true meaning of "love".

14. Why is the rejection of absolute truth primarily a matter of motives? Which of the quotes by famous moral relativists cited on pages 78-79 most affected you, and why?

15. Respond to the quote by Pascal on pages 80-81. Do you agree that this typifies the thinking of most people? Why or why not?

Notes

Notes

3

Some Common Objections... and Some Reasoned Responses

In our contemporary culture many people find the very idea of absolute objective truth to be ludicrous. The assumptions of relativism (including religious pluralism) are absolutely pervasive – even among many Christians and within many churches. Today, nothing could be more controversial or "politically incorrect" than the claim that one's own faith is based on eternal truth. But historic orthodox Christianity has always done just that: uphold the exclusive truth claims of Jesus Christ and the Bible. The question is never, "Is the Christian faith sufficiently sensitive and tolerant according to modern sensibilities?" but "Are the truth-claims of the Christian faith factual and rational?" In other words, are the core beliefs of the Christian faith defensible – including the most foundational doctrine of all: the reality of absolute truth?

Christian Apologetics: The Rules of Engagement

In the context of sharing our Christian faith with others, the use of apologetics requires considerable discernment and spiritual sensitivity. The point, after all, is to speak the truth in love, and this goes far beyond merely regurgitating facts, dazzling others with clever arguments, or trying to control encounters through manipulative tactics or the force of one's personality. At the risk of sounding excessively dramatic, the process of engaging nonbelievers in serious conversation and challenging their misconceptions is a form of spiritual warfare, and we are incapable of doing this effectively if we rely solely on our own personal resources. As in living out the Christian life on a daily basis, we must be enlightened, guided and empowered by the Holy Spirit or else our efforts are ultimately futile and fruitless.

Some Christians are knowledgeable and experienced in using apologetics to engage nonbelievers, and some are naturally sensitive when it comes to tuning in to people's verbal communication and picking up on non-verbal signals. But regardless of how knowledgeable, experienced or sensitive we are, suffice it to say that we can increase our effectiveness and sharpen our discernment through a regular practice of the traditional spiritual disciplines – particularly, the disciplines of study and prayer (both discursive and contemplative prayer).

The connection between apologetics and systematic learning is obvious, but Christians often fail to associate apologetics with prayer and meditation. As we develop a discipline of regular communion with God, we eventually can become more attuned to his nature. As Dallas Willard has written, "It is by stepping experientially into the practices of spiritual transformation... that all the truths about God and his kingdom become truths about your actual existence."* In the process we also explore the depths of our own soul and increase our own self-awareness, which in turn sharpens our awareness and sensitivity to others and their needs. So effective apologetics is like everything else in the Christian life: it is a spiritual practice that requires spiritual discernment.

Some people who we encounter are sincere but misinformed, and their questions and comments should be handled seriously, respectfully, and patiently. Others are closed to the truth and interested in little more than distracting or confusing us. Some questions are honest and deserve a respectful answer while others do not. Unfortunately, some people are so mentally confused or morally perverted as to be beyond our ability to help. Occasionally,

---

* Cited in J.P. Moreland, *Kingdom Triangle: Recover the Christian Mind, Renovate the Soul, Restore the Spirit's Power* (2007), p. 9.

we might even encounter someone who poses a real danger to us and others either physically, psychologically, or spiritually. In certain situations we might need to heed the words of Jesus when he cautioned his disciples, "Do not give that which is sacred to dogs, or throw your pearls to pigs" (Matt. 7:6).

When we endeavor to share our faith with others, there are a few common sense rules of engagement that we are well advised to heed.

- Be patient with those who seem to be honestly and sincerely seeking truth.
- Don't argue or become emotional, and don't take the nonbeliever's skepticism or attacks on the Christian faith personally.
- Don't apologize for what the Bible clearly teaches or try to make the Christian faith correlate to modern humanistic sensibilities and political correctness.
- Stand your ground and don't back down amid pressure, but always share the truth in love as we are exhorted to do in I Peter 3:15: "But let Christ be the Lord of your heart. Always be prepared to give an answer to everyone who asks you to give the reason for the hope that you have. But do this with gentleness and respect."
- Avoid no-win scenarios for which you are unprepared, or situations that are not conducive to a serious and focused discussion of the issues.
- If you do not know the facts or the rationale behind a particular issue, honestly admit it and promise the other party that you will try to research it and get back with him/her.
- Rather than being put in the position of constantly asserting and defending what you believe, learn to shift the burden of proof onto the skeptic. As Greg Koukl emphasizes in his practical book on Christian apologetics, *Tactics: A Game Plan for Discussing Your Christian Convictions*, we can do this by

mastering the technique of asking simple leading questions such as *"What do you mean by that?"* or *"Why do you believe that?"* This can be a very effective way of opening up conversations and exposing the other person's misconceptions about basic moral issues and Christian beliefs in general. As Koukl advises, "Never make a statement – at least at first – when a question will do."

When we ask honest and sincere questions, we show genuine interest in others. Questions are interactive and engaging, and they can be remarkably effective. They provide insight into the other person's character and beliefs, and they force them to think about their assertions. Questions can also help diffuse potentially tense encounters: rather than responding defensively or negatively to fallacious comments, we can challenge the other person to defend his/her assertions by simply inquiring, *"Have you ever thought about...?"* or *"But have you ever considered...?"* or *"Help me understand why you believe that."*

Questions also shift the burden of the argument onto the other person. Asking simple leading questions is an almost effortless way to redirect the conversation in a positive way without coming across as abrupt, negative or defensive. As Koukl notes, "Someone once said if you word the question right, you can win any debate."

Ultimately, we witness to what we believe just as we seek to live what we believe: by faith as we are prompted by the Holy Spirit, whom Jesus promised would lead us into all truth (John 16:13).

Some Common Objections

Any Christian who endeavors to share his/her faith with others can expect to encounter resistance and objections from those who regard Christianity as a form of religious fascism and an annoying impediment to their individual freedom. The following objections are some of the more common arguments that relativists use to try to discredit the Christian faith or otherwise justify their skepticism, but all of these objections ultimately fail. **As Christians, we have the truth on our side. Our challenge is to study and prepare so we can convey the truth as naturally, effectively and persuasively as possible.**

"Your Honor, my client pleads not guilty by reason of cultural relativism."

1. *"There is no absolute truth; everything is merely a matter of opinion."*

Imagine a scenario in which we seek to engage a friend, Paul Postman (i.e., "Postmodern man") in a DPD (Deep Philosophical Discussion). Paul is a typical product of postmodern relativism, and at some point in the exchange he begins to sense that we believe in that old antiquated notion of absolute truth. Furthermore, he begins to suspect that we actually believe that a Biblical worldview corresponds to that truth. In all likelihood Paul will say something like, *"Well, that's fine if you want to believe that, but that's just your opinion. Personally, I don't think there is such a thing as absolute truth; I believe everything is just a matter of opinion."*

Now when people like Paul say something like that, they usually intend it as a dialogue suppressor or as an unsubtle hint to move on and change the subject, but unwittingly Paul has just issued us an open invitation to further engage him on the matter. Little does he suspect that there actually are reasoned answers to his assertion.

When Paul declares, "I don't believe in absolute truth," rather than reply defensively we can simply ask: ***"Oh, why not? Why do you think truth is relative? How did you come to that conclusion?"*** With that, we invite him to clarify and explain his position in an open and non-threatening way. In all likelihood he probably hasn't thought through it to any extent, but we offer him ample time to respond.

At this point, we might follow up by asking: ***"So you think it's true that everything is just a matter of opinion?"*** He'll assure us that yes, there is no such thing as absolute truth, to which we reply: ***"So you're telling me that it is absolutely true that there is no absolute truth? Isn't that an obvious contradiction, like saying that something can be absolutely relative?"*** At this point, Paul might feel like one of those cartoon characters who has just run off the edge of a cliff and momentarily finds himself suspended in mid-air before realizing there is nothing holding him up.

As Paul struggles to regain his composure (or his footing), we can lead him further by saying something like: ***"I, of course, do believe in absolute Truth, and I don't think everything is just a matter of opinion. So why do you prefer your opinion to mine?"***

As Paul attempts to answer the question, we accord him our full attention and listen as perceptively as possible. In a situation like this, if we are honest and sincere and operate in a spirit of humility, we can earn his respect. He might even reciprocate and ask us why we *do* believe in absolute truth, at which point we need to be prepared to defend our view with facts and sound reason.

If Paul persists in arguing that "everyone's entitled to his or her opinion," we might ask: ***"Do you believe people ever have wrong opinions about things? Furthermore, do you think*** *there is anyone doing anything in the world right now that is wrong?"* If he is intellectually honest, he will have to concede that, yes, some people do in fact hold some erroneous opinions about things, and furthermore, there are people doing things in the world right now that are wrong. There are people who are cheating, stealing, deceiving, exploiting, molesting, raping, and murdering others, and these acts are wrong regardless of their motives and opinions. In fact, some people's opinions about right and wrong are more plausible and defensible than others because they are based on facts, sound reasoning, and a clearer understanding of good and evil. If Paul concedes this point, he has admitted that some opinions can be right and others wrong – in which case he has ceased to be a moral relativist.

Furthermore, we can point out: *"If everything is merely relative, why would we ever disagree with another person's opinions or actions? What would it matter if everything is just relative and there is no such thing as truth?"* In which case, why would we ever argue about politics or religion or moral ideas – let alone art, movies, music or sports? But the fact of the matter is that we *do* care about these things, and we care about them precisely because we value what is True, Good and Beautiful. And that goes even for those who claim there is no (absolute) truth.

Now if Paul agrees that some views are more valid than others, he is admitting that some opinions conform more closely to an absolute standard that is above-and-beyond the opinions themselves. In other words, opinions are judged as right or wrong, valid or invalid, according to how they measure up to an objective standard. And that standard, of course, is objective truth.

But what if Paul turns out to be less than intellectually honest? What if he refuses to concede that some opinions are better (i.e., more rational, factual or moral) than others? At that point, we can expose the inherent contradiction in his position by asking: *"But that's just your opinion, right? If everything were relative, that would apply even to your own statement, wouldn't it?"*

At this point it may dawn on Paul that his position is rather transparently untenable, and he may wish that he had opted to take that Philosophy 101: Logic & Critical Thinking course that he by-passed in college. His contention that there is no truth and that one person's opinion is just as valid as another's is a meaningless and inherently self-contradictory position. As the British philosopher Roger Scruton observes, "A person who says that there are no truths, or that all truth is 'merely relative,' is asking you not to believe him. So don't!"

Finally, if given the opportunity, we need to remind Paul that beliefs have consequences. If we sense that he is open to hearing it, we will do him a great favor if we challenge him to seriously consider two things:

(1) *"In the Bible, Jesus made some exclusive truth-claims about himself. In his trial before Pilate, he said: 'I came to testify to the truth.' On another occasion, he declared, 'I am the Way, the Truth, and the Life. No one comes to [God] except through me.'*

He also claimed, 'Whoever believes in me has eternal life,' while those who reject him will experience spiritual death."

(2) *"What if objective truth really exists? What are the consequences if you're wrong? What if Jesus Christ truly is the spiritual savior of humanity? Are you willing to seriously open your heart and ask God to lead you to the truth?"*

At this point, of course, we've taken the issue about as far as we can. The rest is up to Paul. We can only pray for him and make ourselves available in whatever ways we feel led by the Spirit.

2. *"There is no absolute truth. Truth is whatever we accept, or whatever most people believe."*

This assertion, although transparently absurd, is one of the defining premises of postmodernism. In philosophy this is referred to as the **consensus theory of truth**, and there is a rather obvious problem with it. If our friend Paul Postman raises this point, we can expose the irrationality of it by simply asking: ***"But what if I don't believe that truth is decided by majority opinion? Who is right – you or me?"***

If Paul replies that he is right because most people believe the same way he does, point out that there are two problems with this position:

(1) He has contradicted himself in admitting that there is in fact such a thing as absolute truth – i.e., truth is whatever most people believe. However, we should quickly add that we categorically reject the notion that truth is based on consensus.

(2) Ask: ***"Can the majority ever be wrong about something?"*** Of course, he will have to agree that sometimes the majority is wrong, such as in the past when most people still considered racism and slavery and sexism to be morally permissible. This being the case, Paul has conceded that truth cannot be defined by whatever most people happen to believe.

So unless *everyone* believes that "Truth is whatever most people happen to believe " – and of course not everyone does believe it – then this statement is meaningless.

NOTE: There are, of course, situations in which agreement *does* make something true – as with certain civil laws (traffic laws, for instance) and definitions of important words and terms on which there is a consensus agreement. But in many other situations truth is *not* relative or a matter of consensus, such as...

- The geocentric theory of the universe, which was widely held until about 500 years ago;
- The general acceptance of slavery until about 200 years ago;

- The general acceptance of male chauvinism throughout most of world history; or
- The belief that many people hold that a *fetus* is not a "person" in the full sense of the word.

3. "Truth is whatever is practical, or whatever you can get away with."

This argument is even more cynical and transparently dishonest than the previous one, yet many people will resort to it if it suits their purpose. (In fact, many politicians are masters of this deception.) Philosophers call this the **pragmatic (or functional) theory of truth**, and the principle is exemplified in a brief exchange between Jesus and some Jewish leaders in Matthew 21:23-27. As Jesus is teaching in the temple, they approach him and ask, "By what authority are you teaching and healing, and who gave you this authority?" Jesus replies with a question of his own, and tells them that if they will answer his question he will respond to theirs. He then proceeds to ask, *"Did John the Baptist's authority came from God or man?"*

The priests and elders are in a quandary. Everyone knows they actively opposed John's ministry, but John was enormously popular among the common folk. So as they discuss Jesus' question among themselves, they carefully calculate their options. If they concede that John's authority came from God, Jesus will ask why they rejected him; but if they answer that John's authority came from man, the crowd might turn on them because John was regarded as a great prophet. So they simply reply, "We don't know" – to which Jesus responds, "Neither will I tell you by what authority I do these things." He knows they are not sincerely seeking the truth.

Jesus posed a simple question that required his opponents to take a stand on a controversial issue of the day: the legitimacy of John's ministry. The priests and elders were unable to answer honestly because they had no real regard for truth. For them, what really mattered was protecting their own power and status, so everything they said or did was purely based on pragmatic self-interest. Knowing their hearts, Jesus dismissed them with a remark that essentially implied, "I don't waste my time dialoguing with people like you" – thereby heeding his own prior advice when he cautioned his disciples against casting their pearls before swine.

The lesson here for Christians is that some people have no respect for truth nor the capacity to think and function morally. These are the kind of people the apostle Paul referred to in Romans 1 who consciously, deliberately and habitually violate God's moral law, and as a result God has given them over to a reprobate mind. Self-absorbed and ego-driven, they are beyond reason and beyond hope. Their problem is not a lack of understanding but an egregious indifference toward what is right and true.

When we encounter someone who claims that "Truth is whatever you can get others to believe," we can only express honestly and directly what we believe. We might ask: *"You're not really serious that truth is whatever you can get away with, are you?"* If they respond affirmatively, ask: *"What if I purposely deceived you or fed you misinformation? Would you mind? Would it be honest and truthful if I tried to make you believe something that is morally wrong or factually inaccurate?"* If they have any moral conscience at all, they have to respond that of course they would resent it. But if they persist in holding to their immature and irresponsible notion that truth is whatever we can get away with, we should regard them as Jesus did the Pharisees: disengage and stop wasting our time.

4. *"Truth is whatever we sincerely believe."*

If our friend, Paul Postman, opts for this version of relativism, there is considerably more cause for hope than in the previous scenario. We might start by asking him: *"Do you really think you can make something true simply by thinking it is true?"* Unless Paul has recently been watching Deepak Chopra on a PBS special or has fallen under the spell of one of those "Word of

Faith" televangelists on the Trinity Broadcasting Network (TBN), he will probably concede that no, we are bound by the limitations of reality. We can reinforce this assumption by pointing out that the logical Law of Identity defines reality. (See below.)

Some Self-Evident Propositions

Existence (Ontology):
- Something exists.
  - For example: I do.
- Nothing cannot produce something because nothing has no potential to produce something.
- Everything that comes to be is caused.

Knowledge (Epistemology):
- Something can be known.
- Opposites cannot both be true.
- Everything cannot be false.

Logic:
- **Law of Identity.**
  - 'A' is 'A'.
- **Law of Non-contradiction.**
  - 'A' is not non-'A'.
  - 'A' cannot be non-'A' at the same time or in the same relationship.
- **Law of the Excluded Middle.**
  - Either 'A' or non-'A'.
- **Law of Rational Inference.**
  - If 'A' equals 'B' and 'B' equals 'C', then 'A' also equals 'C'.

We can further drive home the point by asking: ***"What if I sincerely believe in objective truth rather than your idea that 'truth is whatever we sincerely believe'? Can we both be right?"*** We are assuming for the sake of argument that Paul is sane and sober, in which case he will have to concede: "Well, *obviously not; if two statements contradict one another, they cannot both be true"* – which takes us back to the arguments related to objection #1 on page 91*ff*.

Some skeptics try to avoid the obvious irrationality of this proposition by asserting that "Something can be true for you, but not for me" – to which we might simply ask: **"Is your statement true only for you, or is it true for everyone? If your statement is true for everyone, then obviously it is not true only for you; on the other hand, if your statement is not true for everyone, then it is self-refuting."**

If something is in fact true, it is *objectively true* regardless of one's subjective feelings or beliefs about it. Imagine a scenario in which one person affirms, *"I believe that God created everything that exists,"* a second person declares, *"I believe there is no God and that matter exists eternally,"* and a third person states, *"I believe we are all God."* Can they all be right? Obviously not, according to the Law of Non-contradiction and the Law of the Excluded Middle (see pages 66-68 and the box on page 98). The fundamental flaw in this argument is that sincerity doesn't make anything true. **The point to be emphasized is that when it comes to the search for truth, sincerity is essential, but it's not sufficient. Facts and reason determine what is true – not sincerity and/or motives.**

5. *"Perhaps there is such a thing as truth, but we can never know it."*

Superficially, this objection sounds more modest and acceptable than the audacious declaration that truth absolutely does not exist – but in fact it is just as irrational. If Paul brings this up, he probably considers it to be a generous concession on his part, so we need to help him see that this is actually not a step toward truth at all. We can do this by simply asking: **"How do you know that we can't know the truth about something? Is it absolutely true that we can't know the truth about something?"** If Paul agrees, he has contradicted himself because he's conceding that it is possible to know the truth about something. On the other hand, if he disagrees, he has contradicted himself because he's admitting that he doesn't know that it's absolutely true that we can't know the truth about something. If he takes the third option and admits that he isn't sure if his statement is true or not, we can reply: ***"Well, then, if you don't know that we can't know the truth about something, then maybe we can – in which case your statement, which is an absolute assertion that we cannot know the truth about something, is fallacious."***

At this point it might be a good idea to let Paul know that we are not trying to entangle him in his own words or make him look foolish; we are merely trying to expose the irrationality of his objections. Our purpose is not to humiliate him but to defeat his erroneous ideas for the sake of truth.

We can proceed to explain that Christians believe that God, in his love for us, has communicated truth – including his purpose for our lives – with sufficient clarity so as to leave no excuse for ignorance. After all, the point of searching for truth is to find it, as the apostle Paul infers in Romans 1-2. What we are talking about here is not a game or an exercise in clever rhetoric.

Many people who argue that truth cannot be known actually mean that it cannot be know with absolute certainty. On this point, it is important to keep in mind that most of what we know and believe in this life is based on faith and probabilities. (By the way: The acceptance of reality based on faith and probabilities includes whether or not you are actually reading this book right now. Perhaps you're only dreaming this, or maybe all of this philosophizing is really just a nightmare! Why should you believe it is real? You can't "prove" it, can you? But on the other hand, there is no good reason to doubt it.) The point here is a simple one: In lieu of evidence that can be verified scientifically or mathematically, we can still have sufficient reason to believe based on certain self-evident truths that only the mentally ill or the morally perverted would doubt. As we will discuss below, reasonable beliefs should not be based on what cannot be doubted but rather on what we have the best reasons to believe – the philosophical principle of **inference to the best explanation**. That is sufficient, and with that we must be content.

6. *"No one is perfect – everyone is fallible – so how can we ever know that we are right about anything?*

There is an instructive little parable from the Desert Fathers that relates to this issue. One day, Abba Arsenius was approached by a man who prided himself as a seeker of truth.

Arsenius said, "If you seek truth, there is one thing you must have above all else."

"Yes, I know," said the man. "An overwhelming passion for it."

"No," replied Arsenius. "An unremitting readiness to admit you may be wrong,"

The lesson is obvious: Humility is the key to wisdom. But the very concept of wisdom presupposes that we can progress from relative ignorance to relative enlightenment because God, who is the source of all truth, is a rewarder of those who earnestly seek him (Hebrews 11:6).

The fact that all of us are human and "To err is human" in no way proves relativism. On the contrary, it actually is an argument *against* relativism for the simple reason that the concept of "error" is grounded in the presupposition that there is an objective standard by which we judge something as erroneous. That standard cannot itself be in error – otherwise, we would never know that the original error is erroneous. So the acknowledgment of the fact that we are imperfect and therefore incapable of perfect clarity regarding right and wrong actually concedes that truth is absolute and not relative.

For Christians, the issue is even clearer. As discussed previously in objection #5, we can be certain that we can know the truth about those things that truly matter in life because a loving God has communicated truth to us with sufficient specificity – including everything for which he will hold us accountable.

7. "Christians who believe in moral absolutes are arrogant, intolerant and close-minded."

This statement, steeped in judgmental cynicism, implies that truth is unattainable, so an honest person must remain perpetually non-committal (or "open-minded") about all things.

When the allegation of arrogance is raised, we can first point out that, yes, some Christians are indeed arrogant, intolerant and close-minded. But Jesus was not, and he alone is our model for character and behavior. The fact that Christians fail to live up to Christ's standards is simply a testimonial to the inherent imperfections of humanity. But otherwise, this argument has no real validity.

In reality, moral values would only be arrogant if we made them up ourselves and tried to pass them off as universal truths. But that is not what Christians do. After all, we believe these values come not from ourselves but from God. That is why we accept them, and it is the very antithesis of arrogance to humbly submit to these truths that we believe have been communicated to us by God *via* the Bible. So we may be wrong, but we certainly are not arrogant.

Next, it is instructive to draw a sharp distinction between "tolerance" and "acceptance" (ref. pp. 61-63). Given a particular situation, it may be necessary and proper to tolerate wrong ideas, inferior standards, or practices with which we disagree, but it is never right to accept them. For example, we should tolerate atheists and Muslims, and we should insist that they be accorded the same basic civil rights as anyone. When such people come into our lives, we might even have the occasion to befriend them and love them – but we would never accept their beliefs. On the contrary, some beliefs and practices should never be tolerated: child molestation or fraudulent business practices, for instance. The very idea of tolerance connotes an absolute moral standard by which we judge certain ideas, practices and lifestyles as "wrong" or "inferior," but we must be clear that tolerance does not mean acceptance.

Some Common Objections... and Some Reasoned Responses 103

If our friend, Paul Postman, should complain that "people who believe in moral absolutes are arrogant, intolerant, and close-minded," we might simply ask him: ***"Don't you hold certain opinions that you think are right and true? Does that necessarily make you arrogant, intolerant and close-minded? And by the way – can't skeptics be just as arrogant and intolerant as Christians?"*** If Paul is honest, he should concede that, yes, skeptics can be just as condescending and judgmental as Christians – in which case we can point out that those who hold honest convictions have no monopoly on arrogance and intolerance. As J. Budziszewski comments:

> Arrogance doesn't come from having convictions about the truth; it comes from having the wrong convictions about how to treat people who don't share it with you. Humility doesn't come from not having any convictions; it comes from having the *right* convictions about the importance of gentleness and respect. [J. Budziszewski, *How To Stay Christian in College* (Think Books, 2004), p. 84.]

So the potential problem in our relations with non-Christians is not our doctrinal and moral convictions but how we relate to those who don't share our beliefs. As the old adage says, "Blessed are the humble, for they shall not be humiliated." If we relate to others in the Spirit of Christ – i.e., if we speak the truth in love and humility – we can disagree without being disagreeable, and our dialogue will not degenerate into a power struggle or a battle of egos.

We might also ask Paul: ***"Do you consider open-mindedness preferable to close-mindedness?"*** Of course he does – relativists always believe it is better to be open-minded than close-minded – in which case we can follow by asking: ***"So you consider open-mindedness to be a virtue?"*** Paul probably doesn't much care for words like "virtues" – he would rather talk about "values" – but nevertheless he will agree that, yes, open-mindedness is a "virtue."

Now we can ask: ***"Would you regard open-mindedness to be an absolute virtue?"*** If he responds, "No, I don't believe in absolutes," we might ask: ***"So when is it better to be close-minded rather than open-minded?"*** At this point, he either has to back-track or acknowledge the reality of absolute truth – in which case he refutes his original charge. If, on the other hand, he replies, "Yes, open-mindedness is an absolute virtue," then he has contradicted his statement that to believe in absolutes is "arrogant, intolerant, and close-minded." We can drive home the point by reminding Paul that, ultimately, open-mindedness cannot be true unless it acknowledges some real absolutes that cannot be denied.

Furthermore, we might resort to the **argument from absurdity** by challenging a moral value or action that Paul cherishes. For instance, we might argue that racism and racial discrimination is justifiable, or that women should not be accorded equal rights, or that homosexuals should be imprisoned. Of course, Paul will argue vehemently that we are wrong, and that there is no moral justification for such sentiments and actions – in which case we can simply ask: ***"But what right do you have trying to impose your values on me? Aren't you being intolerant and close-minded?"*** In this way we expose Paul's relativism for what it is: merely a tactic to avoid dealing with moral issues that he would prefer to ignore rather than a true value that he sincerely and consistently holds.

Finally, we should remind Paul that open-mindedness is no virtue at all if all the facts and logic argue otherwise. We might ask: ***"But what if the absolute view of something is true? Would it be right to continue denying it?"*** We can emphasize that to remain undecided or non-committal when all the facts and logic argue otherwise would be abject foolishness and the epitome of intransigent dogmatism. Furthermore, this misunderstanding of open-mindedness is actually a form of close-mindedness because it refuses to acknowledge that any absolute view of anything is possible.

8. *The "infinite regress of premises" argument.*

Some argue that nothing can be known for certain, and their reasoning is based on the concept known as the "infinite regress of premises." Typically, the syllogism goes like this:

(A) Certainty comes only by adding a reason (or a "proof") to an idea.

(B) However, every proof depends upon its antecedent premise being true.

(C) However, these premises are true only if proved by other (prior) premises, which are themselves true only if proved by the premises that preceded them – *et cetera* and *ad infinitum.*

(D) Therefore, nothing can be absolutely certain because every proof depends upon its premises being true.

The argument that all arguments must have an infinite regress of premises was dispelled by Aristotle more than two thousand years ago in his treatise on metaphysics. According to him, the chain of premises need not stretch back infinitely because it ends at **First Principles – self-evident truths** which need not be proved by prior premises. (Ref. the chart on page 98.) Aristotle based his reasoning on the *a priori* assumption that we can access reality through normal human perception and rational thought, and that therefore certain truths are undeniable. In one of his classic Winnie-the-Pooh stories, A. A. Milne cleverly illustrated this point:

> So [Winnie-the-Pooh] bent down, put his head into the [rabbit] hole, and called out: "Is anyone at home?" There was a sudden scuffling noise from inside the hole, and then silence.
>
> "What I said was, 'Is anybody at home?'" called out Pooh very loudly.
>
> "No!" said a voice; and then added, "You needn't shout so loud. I heard you quite well the first time."
>
> "[But] isn't there anybody here at all?" said Pooh.
>
> "No! Nobody!"

> Winnie-the-Pooh took his head out of the hole, and thought for a little, and he thought to himself, "There *must* be somebody down there, because *somebody* must have said '*Nobody*.'" [A. A. Milne, Winnie-the-Pooh and the Honey Tree (Golden Press Western Publishing Company, 1976).]

Pooh knew intuitively what many intellectuals refuse to acknowledge: that some things are self-evident and need no further evidence or explanation. In *The Abolition of Man*, C. S. Lewis uses an apt illustration to describe the absurdity of the infinite regress argument:

> You cannot go on 'explaining away' forever [or else] you will find that you have explained explanation itself away. You cannot go on 'seeing through' things forever. The whole point of seeing through something is to see something through it. It is good that a window should be transparent, because the street or the garden beyond is opaque. How if you saw through the garden too? It is no use trying to 'see through' first principles. If you see through everything then everything is transparent. But a wholly transparent world is an invisible world. To 'see through' all things is the same as not to see. [C. S. Lewis, The Abolition of Man (HarperSanFrancisco, 1944, 1974, p. 81.]

Lewis makes a fundamental point regarding the search for meaning and truth. The search itself is not the point or the goal. It is not the end, but the means toward the end. There is a point – and an ultimate goal – and we search in order to find that something. That something, of course, is the truth.

So truth is founded on self-evident propositions, or First Principles, that irrefutably correspond to reality. As Aristotle wrote in *Metaphysics*, "Those who wish to succeed [in their search for truth] must ask the right preliminary questions." This is so immanently sensible that only a pseudo-intellectual committed to relativism could miss it. As the philosopher and theologian Norman Geisler observes:

> These self-evident propositions are the foundation for all knowledge.... Truth has an absolute foundation in undeniable first principles and it can be tested through logical means because it ultimately corresponds to reality.
> [Norman Geisler and Ron Brooks, *When Skeptics Ask* (BakerBooks, 1990), p. 272.]

Naturally, there are those who refuse to accept that there are First Principles of truth because they sense that such a concept limits their own autonomy. Therefore, they are resolute in insisting that everything remain open, relative and subjective. Their problem, of course, is not really intellectual but volitional (and probably moral), and such people are typically resistant to reason. (See several notable examples on pages 78-81). Such people may be beyond our ability to convince, although the medieval Muslim philosopher, Avicenna (980-1037), offered up a creative solution to dealing with people like this:

> Those who deny a first principle should be beaten and burned until they admit that to be beaten is not the same as to not be beaten and to be burned is not the same as not to be burned.

A vital corollary to the Law of First Principles is that we need not have absolute proof in order to believe in absolute truth. As noted earlier, truth is that which corresponds to reality, regardless of whether we perceive it or not. Furthermore, we might not like a particular truth, but it is still objectively true in itself regardless of our sentiments.

9. "Many people disagree about truth; therefore, relativism must be true."

This particular argument for relativism is rather obviously fallacious. Just because there are many perspectives on something does not mean that we cannot draw some true conclusions about it. Also, just because truth is difficult and elusive, it does not mean that it does not exist.

This objection is based on a common misunderstanding regarding the nature of disagreement. Disagreement does not prove relativism. It may simply mean that no one has full knowledge of a particular matter, or that some people have faulty assumptions about reality. But disagreement says nothing about the truth or falsehood of an argument.

Disagreement sometimes derives from different cultural backgrounds, but that is irrelevant. The issue still remains the rightness or wrongness of certain beliefs, not their origin. As demonstrated in objection #1, no one thinks that all views are legitimate. Everyone concedes that some views are "more true" than others. Therefore, to admit that something is "more true" is to concede that it correlates more closely to an absolute standard of truth.

Relativists will sometimes resort to the infamous "**Elephant of Truth**" parable in an attempt to illustrate that everything is merely a matter of opinion or perspective.

- Six blind men approached an elephant.
- One man, feeling only the trunk, described the elephant as being like a giant snake.
- Another man felt only the ears and concluded that an elephant is like a fan.
- A third man felt the elephant's massive side and declared that elephants are like walls.
- The fourth man, who was particularly short, encountered the elephant's leg and imagined that elephants are like trees.

Some Common Objections... and Some Reasoned Responses 109

- The fifth man approached the elephant from behind, felt only its tail, and deduced that elephants look like ropes.
- Finally, the last blind man felt only a pointed tusk and assumed that elephants are shaped like spears.

Now, does this simple story prove the point that "Since so many people disagree, relativism must be true?" Is "truth" purely a matter of perspective? Not at all. First, it is important to note that all six blind men were in fact wrong. No doubt, all of them held sincere convictions based on their limited experience with an elephant, but none of their subjective conclusions were in fact true. There is an objective truth about elephants that none of the blind men realized, so the parable really says nothing about truth.

Furthermore, the allegation that "Everything is a matter of perspective" is either an absolute statement, or else it is a relative statement based solely on one's perspective. If it is absolute, then it is not true that all truths are a matter of perspective. If, on the other hand, the statement is merely a matter of perspective, then there is no reason to consider it absolutely true since it is merely the point of view of the one making the assertion. In either situation, the statement is self-refuting, illogical, and untrue. Truth is reality, even if no one fully perceives it or understands it.

10. *"There is no absolute truth; we all create our own reality."*

In a form letter promoting his book, *The Higher Self*, the popular New Age guru Deepak Chopra makes the following assertions:

> Dear Friend:
> You *are* your own reality.
> You create it; you carry it around with you; and most importantly, you project it onto everyone else and everything else you encounter.
> But the traditional Western notion of reality is much too limiting for a true realization of life. If you are to understand yourself and the world around you properly, you need to expand the boundaries of reality – of time, space and matter. Once you've done this, you can align the energy of your physical body with the energy of the universe. In doing this, you tap into an infinite reservoir of intelligence.
> This is the Higher Self. The 'you' inside of you. the living force that knows why you are here on earth, what you need and how to get it. [Quoted in Paul Copan, *That's Just Your Interpretation* (BakerBooks, 2001), p. 36]

Surely, it is true in a limited sense that we create our own reality. Through our choices and actions, we either cause or allow certain things to occur. To an extent, we can alter reality through "the power of positive thinking" – or by the power of a positive (and healthy) lifestyle. Nonetheless, there are definite limitations to our capacity to alter reality just as there are unchangeable realities over which we have no control. As in objection #4, it is important to keep in mind that to believe something sincerely – even passionately – does not make it real. There is a difference between the truth of a belief and the belief itself. Sincerity doesn't alter basic physical and mathematical laws, nor does it alter basic facts or moral laws. Likewise, sincerity cannot change the past any more than wishful thinking can bring someone back from the dead.

11. "Reality is shaped by forces beyond our control."

This contention is the inverse of the previous argument, but probably just as universally accepted. Strangely, although the two premises are contradictory, many people seem to embrace both of them depending upon circumstances.

There are, of course, those who are exclusively committed to this premise. Charles Darwin is quoted as having said, "Wickedness is no more a man's fault than bodily disease." Another example is the Nobel Prize winning geneticist, Francis Crick, who writes in *The Astonishing Hypothesis*:

> The Astonishing Hypothesis is that 'You' – your joys and your sorrows, your memories and your ambitions, your sense of personal identity and free will – are in fact no more than the behavior of a vast assembly of nerve cells and their associated molecules. [Ibid., p. 42]

The influential behavioral psychologist B. F. Skinner made a similar argument in his book, *Walden Two*:

> If I am right about human behavior, I have written the autobiography of a nonperson.... So far as I know, my behavior at any given moment has been nothing more than the product of my genetic endowment, my personal history, and the current setting. [Ibid., p. 43]

What Darwin, Crick, Skinner and others like them advocate is a concept known as **metaphysical determinism** – the idea that we are mere pawns of the biological and sociological forces that control us. They theorize that everything in life is strictly a product of naturalistic cause-and-effect relationships, and that present realities are determined by the past. Karl Marx would have agreed.

As I argued in #10, there is no doubt that unlimited free will is an illusion. We are all impacted by certain conditions and restrictions associated with our DNA, our environment, and our life experiences. No one is 100% rational and objective, just as no one is perfectly mentally healthy. (Of course, it requires a certain degree of mental health to realize that one is not 100% mentally healthy.)

We are all influenced by our heritage, family, culture, education, vocation, friends, beliefs, experiences, and other factors – just as we are also conditioned by our physiology.

Nonetheless, some measure of objectivity and self-determinism is normative and achievable. As beings created in the image of God, we have sufficient self-awareness and free will to make fundamental moral choices. Those who make dogmatic and absolute statements  such as "We are only products of our environment and our genes" seem not to believe that their own opinions are merely products of their environment and their genes. When someone like Crick pontificates that we are "no more than the behavior of a vast assembly of nerve cells and their associated molecules," he conveniently ignores the correlative implication that his own opinion may be "no more than the behavior of a vast assembly of nerve cells." In his delusional hubris, he commits the self-excepting fallacy (see page 68). Presumably, he would like his readers to think that he has somehow transcended the limitations of common humanity to the point that he sees the situation clearly and objectively.

Likewise, there is no reason why we should take Skinner's opinion seriously. After all, it is "nothing more than the product of [his] genetic endowment, [his] personal history, and [his] current setting." The same holds true for someone such as the academician Richard Rorty who claims that nothing can be said about truth "apart from one's own society's descriptions." But why should we take his opinion seriously if it is merely the product of his own socialization? **Pompous intellectuals can be such dimwits. There is nothing, regardless of how erroneous, illogical or absurd, that isn't being taught dogmatically as fact by some narcissistic academician somewhere.**

Metaphysical determinism plagues all areas of scholarship, including my own field of history. Many contemporary historians contend that the study and writing of history is purely subjective. To them, history is little more than a process in which the historian imposes his own biases and agenda on the past. Therefore, history is rendered virtually indistinguishable from myth and propaganda. But of course if this were true, then their own theories of history are nothing more than myth, propaganda, and the imposition of their own subjective biases and agenda on the past.

Fatalism is incompatible with Christian faith which holds that the God of the universe offers spiritual life to those who receive it and submit to his will and purpose for their lives. In the process, our hearts and minds are transformed by the power of the Holy Spirit as we grow progressively Christlike in our thoughts, words and actions. Indisputably, our lives are influenced – or conditioned – by a complex matrix of factors, some of which we understand but others to which we are oblivious. But conditioning is not determining. **As human beings made in the image of God, we have, within certain parameters, a measure of free will. We are not totally helpless and pitiful pawns of forces beyond our control. Otherwise, we could not be held accountable for our moral failings.** In this regard the ancient philosopher Heraclitus put forth a much more enlightened understanding of this issue when he observed that "character is fate."

12. *"In lieu of any scientific proof, the burden of proof is on those who believe in absolute truth. Therefore, skepticism is the sensible default position."*

This is a rather obvious logical fallacy and is easily refuted. In the first place, skepticism is not a neutral position — it is innately partisan. Secondly, we might simply ask: ***"If the burden of proof is always on the one who believes any idea, wouldn't the principle also apply to those who are skeptics? Why must the person expressing Christian faith always be put on the defensive?"***

In fact, there is no scientific method that proves that only the scientific method proves truth. This is merely a philosophical assertion that cannot be verified scientifically because it falls outside the proper purview of science. There are many realities in life that cannot be verified using scientific methodology. Love and hate, faith and doubt, right and wrong – does any sane and honest person doubt that these thoughts and beliefs and emotions are real? Therefore, the premise that we should "Accept only what the scientific method proves" is scientifically unprovable and philosophically absurd.

13. *"Logic is just Western thinking."* *

In the late 1960s Alan Watts, an Anglican clergyman, converted to Buddhism after concluding that Christianity was too theistic, "self-righteous," and incompatible with his Eastern worldview. In particular, he disliked the rationality of Christianity, which he dismissed as "Western logic."

But in order to reject Christianity, Watts had to employ "Western logic." With the understanding that Christianity and Buddhism are intellectually incompatible, he realized that he must choose one over the other. In other words, he had to employ dualistic ("either/or") thinking. Eastern philosophy, on the other hand, typically rejects "either/or" thinking in favor of non-dualism ("both/and"), which is patently illogical and impractical – and certainly unlivable.**

Everyone depends upon the basic laws of logic in order to function normally as human beings. In fact, it is no exaggeration to

---

* In recent decades some radical feminists have argued that logic is merely "male thinking." They contend that women can access truth through their own innate (and presumably superior) sense of intuition.

** Non-dualism (or monism) is not universal in Eastern religions or philosophy. For instance, it is not a basic tenet of Confucianism, Hinayana Buddhism, Jainism, or various forms of pluralistic Hinduism.

say that we could not make it through a single day without thinking and acting logically – and dualistically. Every day, we face countless scenarios in which some options are sensible and others are ill-advised; some are practical and others are impractical; some are better and others are worse; some are right and some are wrong.

The acknowledgment that logic applies to reality is undeniable. To argue otherwise, one would have to make a logical argument. But if it takes a logical argument to deny logic, then the argument is of course self-defeating.

Furthermore, if logic correlates to reality, then we can use it to test certain truth claims about reality. Even relativists believe in truth in that they believe their own ideas are true. For instance, like anyone, they accept the law of non-contradiction – if one proposition contradicts another, they cannot both be true.

Now here is the critical point: **The idea that error exists at all is a concession to the reality of objective truth. Just as blindness presupposes sight, evil presupposes goodness and error presupposes truth. Relativists who refuse to recognize the universality of non-contradictions are either mentally deficient or morally dishonest. As for relativists who acknowledge that the law of non-contradiction is universally valid, objective truth is an unavoidable conclusion – in which case they no longer qualify as relativists.**

14. *"I'm not a Christian, but I'm comfortable with my belief system; it works just fine for me."*

Like many other objections, this assertion is usually intended as a dialogue suppressant. The implication is, "I'm quite satisfied the way I am. Discussion over." But rather than concede, this offers an open opportunity to engage the other party on a deeper level.

As earlier, let us suppose we are dialoguing with our friend, Paul Postman. First, we would want to ask, **"Define what you mean when you say your belief system 'works.'"** In all likelihood, he will respond that he is comfortable with his belief system because of the benefits he derives from it. He may say that it brings him peace, it makes him (relatively) happy, he likes the kind of people who share this beliefs, or his particular group of friends offers a supportive community in which he feels comfortable. He might even declare that his beliefs satisfy his intellectual curiosity more than any other alternative, including Christianity. One thing, however, that he probably will not declare is that his belief system is "the truth." (If so, he has forfeited his credentials as a relativist.)

Next, we might ask: ***"Wouldn't a legitimate belief system correspond to reality? For instance, how does your belief system explain...***
   (a) The origins of the universe?
   (b) The origins of life?
   (c) Ultimate Reality?
   (d) The realities of human nature – both the goodness and the evil within ourselves and other people?
   (e) Our sense of meaning and purpose in this life?
   (f) The existence of morality? and
   (g) What happens when we die?"

Let us be clear: **A belief system that does not correspond to truth and reality, or cannot provide rational, factual, coherent, consistent and comprehensive answers to these questions, is ultimately worthless.** Since all belief systems claim to be true – including the ones that deny the reality of absolute truth – they must provide plausible and satisfactory answers to the perennial issues of life. Otherwise, they fail the truth test. They are, in the final analysis, counterfeit religions and false philosophies. After all, the ultimate criterion is not how a belief system makes us feel or the benefits we derive from it, but is it in fact true? **A belief system "works" – i.e., it is useful and helpful – only to the extent that it helps us relate honestly and truthfully to God, to oneself, to others, and to reality in general.** As human beings we are easily deceived, and what we imagine to be working for us might in fact be working against us. So the issue is primarily, "Is it true?" rather than "Does it seem to work?" or "Does it feel comfortable?"

If a belief system correlates to truth, then it will also "work" in the sense that it will be a source of love, peace, hope, security, and a solid basis for moral living. Christians believe that Jesus Christ is God incarnate, the universal Savior of humanity, "the Way, the Truth, and the Life," and the one Mediator between God and humanity. Christians also believe that the Bible was supernaturally inspired by God and is authoritative in all that it teaches. Other religions contain some truth – but only Biblical faith is *the* (absolute) truth. To varying degrees, other religions contain truth and light, but only to the extent that they correlate to the truth as revealed in Scripture. To the extent that they contradict basic Biblical revelation, they are untrue.

Satan is a master deceiver and a master counterfeiter, and he is delighted when people are lured into false philosophies and religions. Someone may be content with his/her religion and think that it "works" for them in the sense that it offers peace, hope, or a strong support network of like-minded believers. They may be totally sincere about their faith. But if it contradicts the truth of God as revealed in the Bible, it is illegitimate and a source of deception.

The greatest expression of love that a Christian can share with a non-believer is to present as clearly as possible the liberating message of the gospel. If we truly love someone, would we not want to lead them to the saving grace available

through faith in Jesus Christ? Would we not want them to come to a knowledge of the one who declared himself to be "the Way, the Truth, and the Life?"

For followers of Jesus Christ, sharing our faith is not an option. Jesus commands it. Yet in our pluralistic, multi-cultural society, merely quoting Bible verses and relating how our faith has enriched our personal life often does not suffice. As the apostle Peter instructs us, we must "Always be prepared to give an answer to everyone who asks you to give *the reasons* for the hope that you have," and to "do this with gentleness and respect" (I Peter 3:15). In other words: **We must be prepared apologetically, using facts and sound reasoning in addition to our own life experiences, to convince others of the truth of the gospel of Jesus Christ. And of course, we must do this in a spirit of love and humility.**

Christians should keep in mind that when we witness to others, we are not sharing "our truth" but the truth that God has revealed through Scripture. As the apostle Paul wrote to the Roman Christians of his day, "I am not ashamed of the gospel, because it is the power of God for the salvation of everyone who believes" (Romans 1:16). In other words, the gospel – the Good News of Jesus Christ – is simply the truth about Jesus Christ. This is why the gospel has the power to transform lives – because it is aligned with the eternal truth of God. As such, it is the expression of pure love and ultimate reality.

The Absolute Truth About Relativism

The absolute truth about relativism is that it is intellectually and morally bankrupt. It is also the greatest single impediment to an honest search for truth. Relativism is incompatible with Biblical Christianity, and it is the foundation for most of the spiritual deception in contemporary life.

So why is relativism so attractive and so pervasive? There are two reasons. First, we are innately egocentric beings who would like nothing better than to usurp the proper place of God in our own individual universe. Relativism appeals to our narcissistic tendency to create our own reality and define our own morality. Ideally, we would like nothing better than to imagine that we are the captain of our own soul and to let our heart be the final arbiter of right and wrong, good and evil. But second, and just as problematic, is a fundamental misunderstanding of the basic difference between philosophical relativism as it applies to eternal and metaphysical truths as opposed to all things that are temporal, physical, and manmade. To clarify this essential distinction, refer back to "A Note on Relativism and Relational Comparisons: A Lesson from the Great American Pastime" on pages 51-52.

As professing Christians, we either accept the exclusive truth claims of Jesus Christ or we do not. If not, we must ask ourselves: Do I really understand what it means to be a Christian? Do I truly have a personal relationship with God through faith in Christ, or am I merely a nominal Christian based on my association with a particular church or tradition? Just as philosophical relativism is a fraud, there are no "relative Christians." We either believe in Jesus Christ with our whole heart and mind, or else we are spiritually lost – and not relatively, but absolutely.

> *"Be on your guard, and stand firm in the faith.*
> *Be people of courage, and be strong.*
> *Do everything in love." – I Cor. 16:13*

Some Common Objections... and Some Reasoned Responses

Notes

Some Common Objections... and Some Reasoned Responses 121

Questions for Reflection and Discussion

1. Which of the "common sense rules of engagement" listed on pages 89-90 are particularly meaningful to you, and why?

2. In sharing your faith and values with others, have you used some of the techniques that Greg Koukl emphasizes in his book, *Tactics*? If so, what has been your experience with this kind of dialogue?

3. Consider the statement on page 91: "As Christians, we have the truth on our side. Our challenge is to study and prepare so we can convey the truth as naturally, effectively and persuasively as possible." Why do you think that many Christians don't take this calling seriously?

4. Which two of the fourteen common objections have troubled you the most in the past, or which two would you have the most difficulty in addressing, and why?

5. When challenged on some of their basic assumptions, people often say something like, "Well, everything's relative" or "Well, I guess your entitled to your opinion." Typically, they use these kinds of comments as dialogue suppressors. How can we turn such comments into invitations to engage the other person on a deeper and more thoughtful level?

6. Simply stated, what is wrong with the "consensus theory of truth?"

7. Do you agree with this statement: "When it comes to the search for truth, sincerity is absolutely essential, but it's not sufficient." What should be the basis on which we determine whether something is true or not?

8. In what way is the statement, "to err is human," an argument for absolute truth and against relativism?

9. How would you respond to the allegation that Christians who believe in moral absolutes are arrogant, intolerant and close-minded?"

10. Simply stated, what's wrong with the popular "elephant analogy" that relativists often cite as evidence that there is no objective truth?

11. Why is belief in unlimited free will an illusion?
In what sense is metaphysical determinism contrary to the Biblical view of human nature?

12. Why is this statement illogical? "In the absence of scientific proof, the burden of proof is on those who believe in absolute truth; therefore, skepticism is the sensible default position."

13. Why is it illogical to think that science is our only true and objective path to knowledge?

14. Why is it reasonable and essential to assume that a belief system that is true would address the issues listed on page 116?

15. Why is relativism so attractive and so pervasive in our society?

Notes

Notes

An Introduction

Seminars and Forums in
Bibliology
Christian Apologetics
Christian History
Contemporary Cultural Issues
Christian Spiritual Formation
Literature and the Arts

Introduction

In Christian history the name "Areopagus" has often represented the intersection of Christian faith and culture. In first century Athens the Areopagus functioned as a public forum for the exchange of ideas, and it was there that the apostle Paul brought the gospel of Jesus Christ to Europe.

• • • • • • •

While Paul was in Athens, he was greatly distressed to see that the city was full of idols. So he reasoned in the synagogue with the Jews and the God-fearing Greeks, as well as in the marketplace with those who were there.

A group of philosophers began to dispute with him. Some of them asked, "What is this babbler talking about?" Then they brought him to The Areopagus *and said to him, "Would you explain this new teaching that you are presenting? You are bringing strange new ideas to us, and we want to know what they mean."*

Then Paul stood up and said, "Men of Athens! I see that you are very religious. For as I walked around your city and looked at your objects of worship, I found an altar with the inscription, 'To An Unknown God.' Now the one whom you worship as 'Unknown' I am going to proclaim to you...." [Acts 17:16*ff*]

• • • • • • •

Like the apostle Paul in pre-Christian Athens, we in post-Christian America face a culture that is increasingly skeptical, if not blatantly hostile, toward Christian faith and values. The erosion of Christian influence in our society is apparent in every area of modern life from law and politics to business, education, the media, the arts and entertainment, public behavior, and private morality.

Many Christians, however, fail to understand that we are losing the culture war because we have essentially forfeited the intellectual war. Beliefs and values have consequences, and responsible Christians can ill afford to drift along with the cultural currents of our day.

The Areopagus is a Christian education ministry that offers seminars and forums on issues relevant to contemporary Christian life. The mission of the Areopagus is to equip Christians to effectively engage our society and culture with the life-transforming truth and love of Jesus Christ. To this end we offer substantive seminar courses and topical forums that challenge Christians to live in accord with the principles and practices of a wholistic Biblical worldview.

• • • • • • •

Let Christ be the Lord of your heart.
Always be prepared to give an answer
to everyone who asks you to give the reason
for the hope that you have.
But do this with gentleness and respect.
– I Peter 3:15

• • • • • • •

Areopagus Seminars

The Areopagus offers an extensive curriculum of courses for Christians who desire to broaden and deepen their understanding of the Christian faith and contemporary culture. Areopagus seminars are semester-length courses that are taught by gifted instructors, and include topics in Bibliology, Christian history, apologetics, contemporary cultural issues, and Christian spiritual formation.

The core of our Areopagus seminar curriculum is our course on Bibliology based on the book by Jefrey Breshears, *Introduction to Bibliology: What Every Christian Should Know About the Origins,*

Composition, Inspiration, Interpretation, Canonization, and Transmission of the Bible. Unlike conventional Bible studies, this course is designed to help Christians develop a thoughtful philosophy of Scripture so as to more effectively explain and defend why we believe the Bible was divinely-inspired, historically reliable, and doctrinally and morally authoritative.

 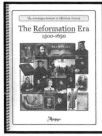 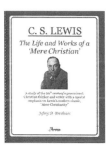 

Our sequence of courses in Christian history cover the major people, issues and events from the time of Christ through the Reformation. We also offer a unique five-course study of Christian history from the founding of America to the present day.

Alternative Universes: A Survey of Comparative Worldviews compares and contrasts a Biblical Christian worldview with alternative worldviews including Deism, Naturalism, Nihilism, Existentialism, Postmodernism, Eastern religions, and the New Age movement.

The Areopagus seminar on Theodicy deals with the philosophical and existential challenges related to reconciling the existence of an omnipotent and good God with all the suffering and evil in our world.

The Historical Quest for the Real Jesus explores the evidence for the historical Jesus of Nazareth and the truth of the Four Gospels along with a critique of the many efforts over the past 2,000 years to reinterpret Jesus to fit various social, political and religious agendas.

Special Topics deals with a variety of theological, historical and philosophical issues ranging from Heaven, Hell, and Near-Death experiences to the fate of those who have never heard of Christ, the debate related to the legitimacy of the Shroud of Turin, etc.

Frontline Apologetics is an interactive study that focuses on how to effectively explain and defend one's values and beliefs on a wide range

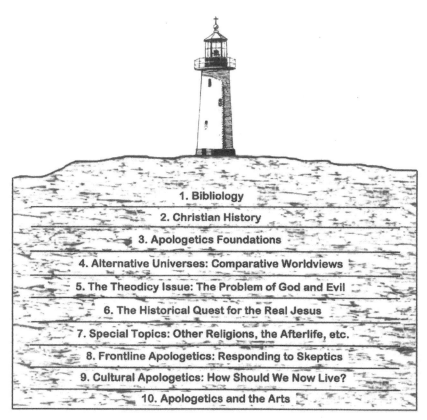

of contemporary issues with Christians who are struggling with their faith, sincere spiritual seekers, and religious skeptics and cynics.

Cultural Apologetics is a three-course sequence that explores in depth the application of a wholistic Christian worldview to the great social, cultural and political issues confronting contemporary Christians in America.

Apologetics and the Arts applies the principles of a wholistic Christian worldview to a thoughtful understanding of contemporary popular culture including movies, music, literature, and the arts.

Areopagus Forums

The Areopagus Forum series features lectures and discussions by outstanding Christian scholars, thinkers and activists on a wide range of topics including cultural and religious issues, apologetics, history, science, Christian spirituality, significant books, and other relevant issues that informed Christians should know.

Forums typically include a formal presentation followed by an extended Q&A session, and offer Christians a unique opportunity to meet and interact with some of the great minds in Christianity today.

  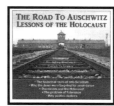 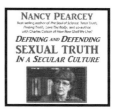

God & the Arts

Popular culture is a pervasive and influential force in contemporary society that has a profound affect on people's values, beliefs and behavior. In that respect, it can either enrich or degrade the quality of our lives and our culture, yet few Christians have a well-developed philosophy (or theology) of the arts.

To that end, the Areopagus sponsors "God & the Arts: Theological Themes in Movies & Music," a series that analyzes the social, political, moral and spiritual content in films and popular music from both an aesthetic and a Christian worldview perspective.

Areopagus Publications

The Areopagus has published a number of books related to bibliology, Christian history and apologetics, and contemporary cultural issues – in addition to numerous study guides and supplemental readings that accompany most of our seminar courses.

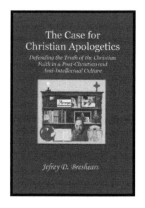
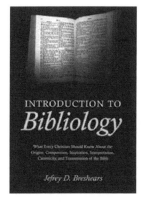

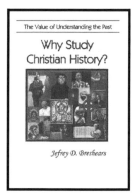

www.TheAreopagus.org
www.facebook.com/theareopagus

Made in the USA
Columbia, SC
13 January 2023

10281434R00080